MEET US
AND
EAT US

FOOD PLANTS FROM AROUND THE WORLD

*Vilma
Bharatan*

Liz Kendall

Vilma Bharatan & Liz Kendall

First published in the United Kingdom in 2024
by The Edge of the Woods
theedgeofthewoods.uk

A CIP catalogue record for this book is available from the British Library.

Printed and bound in the United Kingdom by Gomer Press.

ISBN 978-1-7385570-0-4

Disclaimer
This book is not intended to provide medical or dietary advice; it is not a prescription of what to eat or not eat. It offers an introduction to a small selection of the world's food plants. The information given is not intended to be exhaustive; an entire book could be written about each plant. This book is intended as an entertaining and informative introduction to how a few food plants have travelled the world or stayed at home, and how all have enriched our experience as human beings.

Botanical names change regularly and we have used the most up-to-date at the time of writing.

Contents

Meet Us and Eat Us
Food plants from around the world

Introduction

Food plants: the foundation of life

Plants precede us. Our home planet was once rock, microbes, algae, greenery; flesh lay in the future. Plants are the primary producers, the basis for almost all life on Earth, and most cultures in the world rely on them for food and nourishment. The exceptions usually live in Earth's most extreme landscapes and rely on animals, which can digest plants that humans cannot eat.

In many plant species almost every part can be used for food: stem, leaf, tuber, rhizome, root, flower, bud, seed and fruit. Non-edible parts may have a medicinal use or provide fuel, clothing, or building materials. Plants are more than simply matter. Throughout our history plants have sustained not only our bodies but our imaginations. They are filled with value, with meaning, and with beauty.

The symbolic meaning of food plants is crucial to the imaginative currency of the world's storytelling, art, and spiritual traditions. It is often in myths and fairy tales that we meet potent plants and foods for the first time: the temptations of gingerbread, the deceptive purity of apples, the tiny pomegranate and sesame seeds that unlock hidden worlds. These tales give instruction, warnings, and wisdom. Stories and songs pass on the ritual-spiritual, magical-medicinal, and nutritional-culinary wealth of plants to the next generation.

Poetry tells us that love begins in the eyes, at first sight; the workaday world says it is kindled in the stomach. When the eyes and stomach are wooed together it is an irresistible combination: the heart lies in between. Modern gift-giving is still reliant on flowers, special foods, sweets, and alcohol; all plant-based ways to wish someone well or declare love. We still celebrate the seasons through significant plants, from pumpkins (edible) to mistletoe (most definitely not - but it has medicinal use).

Food plant families

Plants, like humans, grow in extended families. Knowing the relatives of the plants you have purchased or picked helps you know what to do with them. Sometimes this knowledge is transmitted in reverse; we grow up with classic recipes without knowing that we are eating a family of plants. Potatoes, tomatoes, aubergines, chillies; they're all from the *Solanaceae* family.

Botanically, the clue to find out how closely related plants are lies in their names. Names are essential to allow us to communicate. Each species, or family member, has two names: the first is the genus and the second the specific epithet. So the tubers of potatoes (*Solanum tuberosum*) and the fruit of aubergines (*Solanum melongena*) are more closely related to one another than either is to the fruit of chillies (*Capsicum annuum*), but all belong to the family *Solanaceae*.

We don't learn much botany in childhood. There is more emphasis on animals and their environments, perhaps a little cooking or gardening, but not much about what keeps it all going: the soil and the food plants that grow there. This book is a chance to join the dots between botany and other disciplines in an accessible way that relates to our everyday food choices.

Understanding taxonomy or the naming of plants enables people not just to understand their characteristics and relationships, but to stay connected to the reality of what food is. Knowing the correct botanical names allows us to find out more about a plant, connecting us with the knowledge base we have accumulated through generations. Recognising food plants in their unprocessed forms (the whole carrot, not just conveniently cut batons), and in all their variety, helps us make connections and choices that can have a positive impact not only on our own health, but also that of the planet.

Children can remember a host of dinosaur names: the spellings, the shapes of the beasts, their individual strengths and weaknesses. This is a glorious testament to the excitement, intelligence, memory and expertise of passionate childhood. This is what we should all protect within us as adults. However, very few children are taught the botanical names of the plants they eat, which is why we've included these names in the book. We have confidence in the sophistication of children's interests. Children and adults can enjoy becoming well-versed in unexpected topics, and plant trivia is not trivial, but keeps us healthy every day.

Food variety is food security

Just like siblings, different varieties of the same species may look and behave quite differently. One may be full of vitality and flavour, another rather dull; one may be large, another a mere sliver by comparison. Since none of us choose our relations, don't write off any plant or be tempted to judge a fruit by its brother. You may dislike one sibling but fall in love with another.

Sometimes we are hoodwinked by marketing and market forces. Often a plant becomes a supermarket sensation, a celebrity in isolation, while the importance of variety, seasonality and freshness are overlooked. Naturally occurring variety along with seasonal or forced growth can alter the nutritional content as well as the taste of what's on your plate. Not all potatoes are created equal.

Variation within a species can happen naturally or through cultivation. When a plant interacts with its environment over time it adapts to changes in the soil, weather, altitude and other naturally occurring variables. Human intervention produces cultivated varieties through selective breeding, and nowadays these are chosen for intensive monoculture farming. This not only diminishes biodiversity through the exclusion of other species, but leads to vulnerability to disease and environmental stresses.

When a vast area is planted with a monoculture, even one change in the environment can result in catastrophic crop failure. The impact of climate change increases this risk. When many varieties are grown, some may prove more resistant than others to climate change, individual diseases or pests; there is less chance of losing the whole harvest. Biodiversity provides disease resistance and crop resilience.

Intensive monoculture farming relies heavily on artificial fertilisers and toxic chemicals, and leaves the soil depleted, which contributes to the degeneration of nutrient content in plants. Even foods that look good can be lacking in essential vitamins, minerals and trace elements. An apple that's been bred large and glossy to catch the eye at the supermarket isn't necessarily the most delicious or nutritious. What we choose to buy and put into our mouths determines what is put into the soil. As poet and environmentalist Wendell Berry stated "eating is an agricultural act" and has the power to change a country's economic, social, political and environmental policies.

It is our limited diets that demand intensive monoculture farming and contribute to global malnutrition. "We oversimplified and disregarded the infinite complexity of nature." (Campbell & Campbell) Currently, 15 plants provide

90% of our food energy. Wheat, rice and maize are the staple diet of four billion people. We are continually narrowing the range of cultivation and this makes the whole world vulnerable. Yet there are thousands of underutilised species of plants and fungi with the potential to feed millions of people productively, as well as providing alternative fuels, fibres for clothing, and materials for housing. We have included a few of them in *Meet Us and Eat Us*.

Travel, while a joy, is not a necessity in eating one's way around the globe. You don't have to spend a fortune on imported exotics to eat well. Many plants we may consider native are immigrants, once an expensive novelty and now an affordable staple, such as potatoes and tomatoes in the UK. We have an ongoing opportunity to choose a wider variety of plants from around the world that will thrive in our climatic conditions. From rare finds to garden regulars, be on the lookout for what is available, affordable, and attractive to you.

You are the secret ingredient

Art and science never used to be separate. Scientific proof and what is known as a fact changes year by year. It's really very important that we remember this. It's not long since most people believed that margarine was a healthier choice than butter. New studies are continually shifting the boundaries of what we know (or what we know for now). So we're not offering a suggested diet or specific foodie lifestyle. We're just showing, through food plants, how art and science nourish one another in a continual act of cross-pollination.

Plants make their own food through photosynthesis. They use the energy from the sun to convert water and carbon dioxide into simple sugars which they use or store. This transfer of energy is the nutritional basis for life, feeding humans and animals (some of which feed humans). The health of plants depends on the soil in which they grow. The soil is full of microbes and they're inside us too: the essential microorganisms in our gut. It is a symbiotic relationship: a cooperative living network between the microorganisms in the soil, the plants growing from it, and what we eat; a constant exchange of nutrients, energy and information.

We have evolved to eat a wide variety of plants as they become available through the changing seasons. Growing and eating different foods throughout the year supports a greater volume and wider variety of microorganisms in our gut. Collectively they are known as the microbiome, and there is increasing evidence that a huge portion of our immune system is found here. When we eat the same few foods all year round, or elevate one plant to "superfood" status, we do so at the expense of its relatives and our own immunity. Variety is the key; the bridge that connects what we eat to our internal microbiome, and enables our immune system to respond to seasonal challenges by giving us a broad spectrum of immunity.

We are part of a vast network of connection and continuing evolution. To take anything out of context or see it as separate is unscientific; we can't afford to pretend these relationships don't exist. If a single berry or spice is being trumpeted as a health saviour, we are forgetting how food works. If the climate changes on one continent, it will eventually affect our own home. Food, which engages all our senses, invites us to stop fooling ourselves and truly experience our interrelationship with all life on earth. Unless we have a medical reason to restrict what we eat, let's rediscover our willingness to play and explore; to absorb all the nutrients, textures, flavours and energy sources we can.

When cooking we have the opportunity to let our senses guide us. We become the secret ingredient. We experience pauses within a state of flow. We can look at the shape of the plant, letting its form suggest how to prepare it. When we peel an onion we can't escape its immediate effect on our senses. We decide whether to slice thin or thick, to chop in rough chunks or finely. At the same time, we make sure we don't chop our fingers off, using dexterity and judgement; all our faculties working together around the watering of our eyes and nose. This is a process in continuum as life is, constantly shifting and changing and asking us to use our senses, our physical and mental ingenuity, to create something that will feed us and keep us going until hunger prompts us again.

Where art and science meet there is joy, understanding and inclusion. We become the secret ingredient bridging these realms.

Trusting our senses, including common sense

Plants keep us alive and well but many can both heal and harm. In edible species, toxins can develop with age or careless storage. Even a plant in its prime can tell us when indulgence has slipped into overindulgence, reminding us that the difference between a medicine and a poison is the dose. The Temple of Apollo at Delphi bore the legends "know thyself" and "nothing in excess". The former will help you judge the latter. It is easy to become overwhelmed by food trends and nutritional ideologies, by piecemeal information and optimistic diets convincing you to cut things out rather than embrace the world of food plants at your fingertips. Cutting something out comes at a cost if we replace it with something else which may not be the best choice. The best food is the best *for you*, so get curious about yourself and notice how different foods make you feel.

It's getting harder to keep it simple and eat sensibly. People are forgetting what food is. Natural foods are those we buy whole, such as raw vegetables, or which are only lightly prepared for sale, such as dried pulses and rice. Manufactured foods are more highly processed, with natural ingredients that have been changed and re-formed into different components. New to our food chain are processing aids, often undeclared and of synthetic origin. These are used to break ingredients down, hold them in their new shape, and prevent decay at the natural rate. The language of labels emphasises plant-based or natural ingredients. It lists the rest of the matter bulking up the meal without explaining its purpose. Processing aids, the most sophisticated items, are not listed at all.

Even when cooking from scratch, you can't tell what has been sprayed on your fruits and vegetables by looking at them. Production costs are being cut and shelf lives extended in a way that is not always declared on the label. So much of our food is invisible these days: invisible by design. Without knowing, we eat hidden additives, unlisted enzymes, improvers, and synthetics masquerading under natural-sounding names. They sneak into everyday packaged food unheralded.

These silent squatters can make their presence felt as joint pain, inflammation and other chronic irritations that are hard to diagnose. The public may be on familiar terms with the latest "superfood" or culinary trend, but know nothing about the changes to the manufactured citric acid in their tinned foods and how this affects their health. Extending shelf life does not keep food at its best, it just keeps it from going off at its natural rate of decay. Old food pumped full of preservatives is still old food past its prime and, when we eat, our organs absorb the preservatives as well as the nutrients. Is it necessary to ingest these ingredients?

Who wants to eat a cake made fourteen months ago? Who convinced us that was desirable, and brought such products onto our shelves? When it comes to convenience foods we have been infantilised and made ill by decades of experimentation. Some recent intrusions, such as glucose-fructose syrup (mass produced from the monocultures of soya or corn), are addictive. Nutritional poverty has increased as a result of fast food. Nowadays we are so well fed but badly nourished. Instead of ensuring that everyone has access to affordable fresh food and the knowledge of how to cook it, we have been swamped by packets promising a quick fix and delivering a slow decline.

So it's time to rely on our senses and common sense. To remember that the more we process a plant, the less of its nutrients we receive. To remember that if we deplete the soil and kill off pollinators, we are damaging the cells of our own bodies. When we eat foods packed with pesticides designed to kill off the creatures living on the plants, regardless of whether they're helping or harming, we also kill off the beneficial microorganisms within our gut, our microbiome. We damage our immune system, the foundation of our health.

Whenever possible, if we can make choices that encourage farming, growing and buying with a forager's heart, we will be nurturing our own survival in relationship with the plants, soil and environment on whose energy we rely.

Why do we swallow the sales pitch that one individual berry species is a "superfood" when all its edible relatives are bright and beneficial? If we have been seduced by the shiny regimental rows of the standardised, then it's time to get down to core truths. To try different varieties, embracing lumps and bumps and idiosyncratic shapes as proof of plants responding to their environment.

Shifting boundaries

Terms like clean or dirty eating, healthy or unhealthy food, and plant-based, don't always bring clarity. Food fads evangelise one isolated vitamin or plant at a time, and the following month the recommendations change again. These trends reduce our ability to think for ourselves and to make individual choices.

We have divorced food from its complex context by looking for a plan and not a poetry of eating. This has led us into the situation "that we are poorly suited to the diets we currently choose" (Campbell & Campbell). It's time to shift the boundaries in our brains from these deceptively simple judgements back to the beautiful complexity of nature, where everything works together.

Plants themselves are an example of shifting boundaries. When we eat a plant or parts of it, we do so at different stages of its transformation. From the whole plant we select roots, tubers, stolons, rhizomes, stems, leaves, buds, flowers, stamens, pollen, and so on. We may see these parts as discrete entities, but they all have a common origin and are growing with intricate symbiotic relationships that we do not see.

In this book we reach across disciplinary boundaries. We have poetry in a range of tones and styles. We have prose to give information in another way, with more details. We have fine art combining photography, illustration, storytelling and design that helps you recognise edible plants and celebrate them in their own right, not just as ingredients. There's a playfulness in how it all fits together.

Making the book accessible to children keeps us connected to a different kind of simplicity; not simple because it's lacking complexity, but because it's rooted

in reality. By including anthropomorphic graphics and poems we invite readers
of all ages to see plants as active partners, worthy of our attention. We remind
ourselves of the part humans played in taking plants to new environments
and creating new varieties. Understanding these connections encourages more
sustainable choices. So *Meet Us and Eat Us* is integrating science, art, and poetry
into a storytelling narrative which travels the world and encourages us to explore.

We thrive in this world when we let ourselves play;
Create an adventure in small ways in each day.
Discoveries don't have to come from hard toil;
There's wildness inside us and rooted in soil.

So sharpen your senses and your instincts too,
And notice which plants seem to call out to you
As you travel these pages and meet some new friends;
These food plants of Earth, on which all life depends.

Beetroot and Swiss chard

Botanical name
Beta vulgaris L.

Common names
(garden beet group)
beetroot
(leaf beet group)
Swiss chard, spinach beet,
leaf beet

Origin and native distribution
Middle East, Europe

Parts used
roots, leaves

Two varieties of *Beta vulgaris*: Swiss chard with their substantial
dark green leaves and broad white leaf stalks (which can be
bright yellow, red, orange or pink) flanked by the swollen
dark red beetroots with their edible leaves.

Beetroot (garden beet group) - *Beta vulgaris*

Can you metabolise red betalain?
What do those words mean? I'll try to explain.
Metabolise means you can use
The nutrients that hide in food.
Red betalain makes beetroot's blood-dark hue
A gorgeous plateful, but quite shocking too.
If startled when your wee flows pink
Consider recent meals, just think.

Have you been eating beetroot soup, rich borsch?
Did you have beetroot salad, fritters, sauce?
Have you been feasting from the jar
Of beetroots in sharp vinegar?
It may be that your body cannot hold
Or utilise those betalains so bold.
But relish their sweet, earthy taste,
Whatever happens to your waste.

Swiss chard (leaf beet group) - *Beta vulgaris*

A forest of rainbows held in your hands,
A bouquet that blooms upside down.
Or moon-struck trunks leading your eyes up and up
To green tender leaves at the crown.
Gather armfuls of *Beta vulgaris*,
Whether white, orange, yellow or red,
For sweet juicy salads, or let colours run
In the heat or the water instead.
Some family heirlooms are jewels,
Small treasures passed on down the years.
Some chards have been with us for five centuries,
For each generation that appears.

The cultivation of *Beta vulgaris* goes back to around 900 BCE when they were part of the Assyrian diet. Several cultivars share a common ancestor native to the coasts of Western Asia and Europe. This wild plant, *Beta vulgaris* var. *maritima*, has been cultivated to produce sugar beet, from which sugar is made, and the vegetables beetroot, spinach beet or leaf beet, and Swiss chard.

The broad, fleshy leaves of all three vegetables can be cooked like spinach, in sauces, soups, and tarts, but are strong enough to use as edible food parcel wrappers. Like other dark green leaves they are rich in iron, along with other minerals such as calcium, magnesium, phosphorous and potassium, and vitamin A.

Beetroot is the only variety to grow rounded roots; these are known for their deep red hue, but they can also be golden yellow. Spinach beet resembles spinach, with pale stalks but wide leaves like Swiss chard. The long stems of Swiss chard can be white or a bright spectrum of colours. Their betalain pigments are soluble in water, so boiling is best avoided. The stalks can be separated from their leaves and braised, or cooked quickly like asparagus. The 16th century produced some colourful heirloom varieties that we still enjoy today.

Betalains are water-soluble bioactive pigments, red to purple and yellow to orange in colour. They are found only in some plant families in the order Caryophyllales and in some fungi, notably members of the Basidiomycota (mushrooms). Caryophyllales includes the families of spinach and beets, and cacti fruits such as prickly pear and dragon fruit. Betalains are widely used to make the natural red colouring E162 for food, cosmetics and pharmaceuticals. The pigments are named after the *Beta vulgaris*, as they were first extracted from the common beet.

Not everyone can metabolise betalain pigments, and when it comes to beetroot it doesn't take long to find out. A small percentage of people will find their urine and stools turning red after eating beetroot, but this isn't harmful, and the root is full of other nutrients that will be absorbed and used. The plant provides vitamin C, iron, folic acid, and tyrosine which benefits the immune system.

Beetroot gives a fantastic shocking pink colour to risottos and sauces. The roots can be eaten raw or cooked. Their earthy sweet flavour works in desserts as well as savoury dishes, and their hard texture means they can be grated, cubed, sliced or cooked whole. Once softened by heat they can be pureed into dips. Roasting or sautéing preserves more of the phytonutrients. If boiling beetroots, wash them well first so that the betalain-infused cooking water can be used as a stock or a drink.

Beetroot is an important vegetable in Eastern Europe and Russia, an essential ingredient in borsch soup or stew. In the Middle East beetroot or its juice is used to colour pickles. Beetroot juice or powdered beetroot is widely used for colouring and flavouring prepared foods, including confectionery. Beetroot itself is often pickled in vinegar. The leaves can be eaten in salads or cooked dishes, so a bunch of beetroot with leaves attached gives scope for more than one dish.

Beetroots marry well with earthy spices such as cumin, fennel, caraway and chilli in soups and stews. Roasted, peeled and sliced for a salad, their sweetness provides a pleasing contrast with the sharpness of lemon juice or balsamic vinegar, goat's cheese or feta, with chopped walnuts or hazelnuts to add texture.

When peeling and preparing beetroot, wear an apron. These leaky roots are worse than pomegranates for making the kitchen look like a crime scene.

Amaryllidaceae family
Garlic, leek and wild garlic

Botanical name
Allium sativum L.

Common name
garlic

Origin and native distribution
Central Asia, Middle East

Parts used
bulbs

Botanical name
Allium ampeloprasum L.

Common name
leek

Origin and native distribution
Eurasia, North Africa

Parts used
leaves, stalks

Botanical name
Allium ursinum L.

Common names
wild garlic, ramsons

Origin and native distribution
Europe, Asia

Parts used
leaves, flowers

Close relatives together: leek, garlic and wild garlic.

Garlic - *Allium sativum*

Great warriors of old could well wield a spear
(That's a sharp point fixed onto a stick).
Anglo-Saxons named me for this weapon of fear
As *spear-leek*, or in their tongue *gar-leac*.

And am I so warlike? Just bring on a foe
Like infection, sore throat or a cough.
Allium sativum brave is quite happy to go
And fight those bacteria off.

I am fearsome when raw, even sweetened with honey.
My chemicals sulphur and allicin bold
Are heroic but will leave your breath smelling funny:
Dragon breath but who cares? Your health is pure gold.

When my spear-headed bulbs lend their strength to your food
Giving flavour that lasts for long hours,
You'll remember I'm fighting blood-battles for you
With my tasty medicinal powers.

Leek - *Allium ampeloprasum*

The housemaids of Sumeria
Had tricks of trade to share.
They found that leeks were useful tools
To purify the air.

It wasn't smells they sought to cleanse
With leek's potent bouquet,
But with its juice in water pots
They kept the flies away.

So wash the windows of your home
With leek-water, and see
How flies avoid your window panes
And keep your life fly-free.

Garlic, leeks, and ramsons or wild garlic are relatives of onion, chives and scallions or spring onions. All share the strong pungent flavour and scent that comes from their sulphurous compounds.

Garlic - *Allium sativum*

Gar is the Anglo-Saxon word for *spear*, *leac* means *leek* or *plant*, and *lic* means *like*, as in *cynelic* meaning *kingly, royal*. So garlic is both spear-leek and spear-like, depending on the chain of etymology. The shape of garlic's cloves and bulb resemble the swelling pointed tip of a spear head, an important symbol and weapon for the Anglo-Saxons.

Garlic has medicinal uses as well as culinary ones, and is a traditional remedy against infections. Recipes for using garlic to stave off colds, sore throats and coughs include eating raw minced garlic or making garlic-infused honey as a more soothing way to take it. In Britain, garlic supplements have been shown to reduce colds by half and the active ingredient allicin is being explored for its medical potential in fighting bacterial infections. Garlic also boosts the circulation.

Garlic's protective powers extend to horticulture, and it is used to poison slugs and prevent root rot in runner beans. It has also been used as a charm to ward off the mythological threat of vampires and trolls.

When we eat garlic, the sulphurous compounds that give garlic its flavour and scent are excreted by the body through our lungs, so our breath becomes pungent.

Garlic is often cooked together with onions, but its small dense cloves contain less water and more fructose. This means that garlic will caramelise and then burn more quickly, so the onions should be given a head start and the garlic added a little later.

Leek - *Allium ampeloprasum*

Leeks were brought to Britain by the Romans and there are many different cultivars grown.

Leeks are long vegetables with tightly layered green leaves growing straight from the white bulb. To encourage more of this white part they can be grown in trenches. In cooking, they are often sliced finely widthways to give slim oval rings. Leek soups include French vichyssoise which pairs leek with potato, and Scottish cock-a-leekie which is traditionally made with chicken stock and prunes.

The leek became a national emblem of Wales when Welsh soldiers wore leeks in their helmets to recognise one another during the battle in which King Cadwallader achieved victory over the Saxons in 640 CE. One popular Welsh recipe is Glamorgan sausages, made without meat, and using leeks, cheese, and breadcrumbs as the main ingredients.

Harnessing the insect-repelling qualities of the *Allium* family, the Sumerians infused water with leeks before washing their windows, to prevent flies from invading their homes.

The leaves and white stalks of leeks can be cooked as a vegetable, served in a cheese sauce, and used to flavour other foods; they are milder than most onions. The white stalk can be thinly sliced and eaten raw in salads. The sprouted seeds are also eaten, as are those of onion and garlic.

Wild garlic, ramsons - *Allium ursinum*

Wild garlic or ramsons are often smelled on the air before they are seen; in April and May the damp woodlands of Europe and Asia are carpeted with their long flowing green leaves and clusters of white star-like flowers. As with all wild foods, they should be foraged with care and respect, ensuring that no area is depleted, as this could damage their growth the following year.

The leaves are mild enough to eat raw in a salad, in sandwiches, omelettes and sauces. They can be chopped up and mixed into butter or made into pesto. They can be dried in a low-heated oven and crumbled for use as a herb. Wild garlic's flavour mellows during cooking.

The active ingredient allicin in wild garlic and its relative bulb garlic lowers cholesterol, and in the Arran Isles it was traditionally used as a remedy for blood clots.

Amaryllidaceae family
Onion

Botanical name
Allium cepa L.

Common name
onion

Origin and native distribution
Central Asia, Middle East

Parts used
bulbs

Red and white onions cheerfully clothed in their papery skins.

Onion - *Allium cepa*

Rotund bulbs of plenty - now why are you crying?
Full-flavoured and pungent - tell me why you're crying!
With slow heat we'll sweeten and caramelise,
So why are you crying? Cheer up!

All countries adore us - I see you're still crying.
A savoury treasury - why are you still crying?
Raw, cooked, white, red, dried, shallot; even our skins
Give a golden brown dye - so cheer up!

Layer by layer, scale by scale, these rings aren't just for frying:
They're your immune system's true friend when you're trying
To escape from infections; viral and fungal too.
So chop *Allium cepa* - cheer up!

Our scent rises to greet you - although you're still crying.
To wake up the chef in you - now try to stop crying.
An aroma of sulphur hits you straight in the eyes,
Surely that's not the problem? Cheer up!

Onions are a feisty bunch whose eye-watering strength of flavour and scent is due to the chemicals they produce in self-defence. They originated in the Middle East and their recorded history goes back at least 3,000 years; they were popular with the ancient Egyptians. They are one of the most widely cultivated plants, and an essential ingredient in cuisines around the world.

Onion's bulb shape is formed by overlapping leaf bases, allowing its scales or layers to be peeled apart, sliced into rings or segments, chopped or finely diced. The method of slicing or chopping affects the flavour, as different surface areas are presented to the heat. Onion bulbs are eaten raw, cooked, dried, or pickled. Their sharply pungent, sweet, or caramelised flavours can be showcased by varied cooking processes. Onions are used to give flavour to other foods and dishes, and the sprouted seeds are also eaten.

Onions are famous for their lachrymatory factor: their power to make us cry. Their chemical self-defence system includes a sulphur molecule that is released into the air when the tissue of the onion is damaged. This hits the eyes and nasal passages of the assailant, making their eyes water. For small assailants like insects and animals, this sulphur spray is enough to put them off after the first bite, but humans proved perversely stimulated by the onion's fierce nature. Shallots, scallions, garlic and leeks share this chemical system, and their various sulphur chemicals produce their individual flavours.

The chemicals which onions developed to ward off animals also kill microbes, and humans have found medical uses for this potency. The antifungal and antibacterial properties of onions have been used in traditional remedies, for example to treat coughs and chest complaints.

The peels or skins of onions have also been put to use, producing a brown dye for clothing. Onion peels can also be used to give a smoky flavouring to gourmet foods and to colour eggs cooked in their shells.

It is when using fresh onions that we receive their best flavour and immune-boosting properties. When onions (and their relatives such as garlic, shallots, and leeks) are old they lose their chemical potency. Dried onion powder will never have the bold flavour punch of the freshly cut bulb. However, in factories where processed food is manufactured, and in some restaurants keen to save time, fresh onion is not used. Instead, pre-peeled frozen onion from the EU or China is bought in. Sometimes this product has already been sent to another factory to be defrosted, chopped or puréed, and re-frozen, with synthetic chemical texturisers added to keep the onions recognisable.

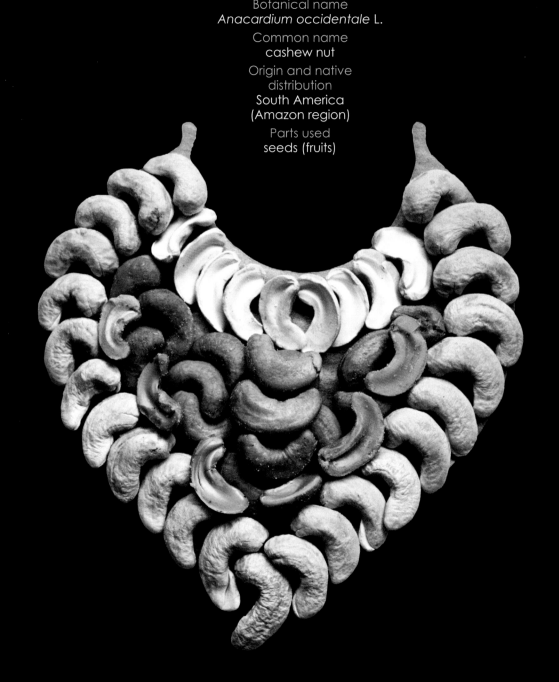

Botanical name
Anacardium occidentale L.
Common name
cashew nut
Origin and native
distribution
South America
(Amazon region)
Parts used
seeds (fruits)

Brazilian whole and split cashew nuts. Darker roasted nuts in the centre
are surrounded by paler raw nuts.

Cashew nut - *Anacardium occidentale*

I'm shaped like a comma,
A pause to take breath,
To stop and to think what you're doing.
I punish the hasty;
The oil I exude
Means each harvest can blister the skin.

A strange sight when growing;
A long apple shape
With one kidney or comma below.
One nut and one apple,
One crunchy, one soft,
My drupe hangs dull; fruit ripens and glows.

Nuts thicken your curry,
Blitz into butter,
Taste moreish with salt or with honey.
But mind you remember
The skin and the fire;
It's safer to pick me with money.

The cashew tree, an evergreen, is a relative of mangoes, pistachios, sumac and poison ivy. Cashews are native to the Amazonian region of Northern Brazil and Southern Venezuela, and they grow well in the dry tropics. They have a long history of use by the indigenous people of Brazil as the tree provided food, firewood and medicines. Once the Americas had been colonised by Europeans, the Portuguese took cashews to India and Africa where they flourished; these countries now produce most of the world's cashew crops. Brazilian varieties are the largest, and have a softer texture than the smaller Indian and African varieties. Vietnamese cashews are almost white in colour with a distinctive sweetness and crunch.

The cashew is a master of disguise, a chameleon, and a nightmare to categorise. It seems to have rummaged through the botanical dressing-up box while blindfolded. Here are a few of its quirks:

The part that looks like a fruit, feels like a fruit, tastes like a fruit, is used like a fruit, and is called an apple, is not a fruit at all. The vibrant yellow or red fleshy pear-shaped structure above the drupe is known as the cashew apple, but is really the flower stalk which swells and expands. Cashew apples can grow to up to 11 centimetres in length. They are sweet and fragrant, and are especially valued in Brazil and India, where they are fermented into wine and liqueur. They are also eaten fresh, used to make pickles, chutneys, jams, candied fruits, vinegar, and juice - just like fruits are. But they are swollen flower stalks and not fruits.

The true fruit of the cashew tree is the hard drupe. This is the smaller, smooth-skinned, kidney-shaped structure that hangs like a swollen comma below the cashew apple. It starts green and turns an ashy brown when mature. The drupe forms before the cashew apple, and the flower stalk swells in order to cushion and protect this prima donna. Inside the drupe grows a single seed kernel, the cashew nut.

The drupe, though a fruit, is as hard as a nut. It is dangerous to eat as the seed kernel is protected by a double-walled fortress of hard shell, between which lurks a layer of caustic liquid or resin. Before reaching the consumer, cashew drupes are roasted to burn off the oil, allowing the delicious seed kernels to be safely extracted and sold. The need for such careful handling makes harvesting cashews dangerous and labour-intensive, which adds to the cost of the end product. Buying certified Fairtrade cashew nuts is a way to ensure that the workers have been provided with protective equipment such as gloves. There are many permanent and painful injuries among workers whose welfare is sacrificed in order to produce cheap cashews.

Cashew nuts are starchy, making them an excellent thickener for curries, stews, soups, and the traditional milky desserts of India. Their sweet nutty taste blends well with cardamom, carrots, coconut, mango, milk and sweet spices.

The caustic cashew nut shell liquid (CNSL) is very useful away from the culinary world. This agricultural waste product is an example of a plant-based renewable alternative to non-renewable products based on fossil fuels. CNSL has uses in engineering, in vehicle and machinery maintenance, in paints and varnishes, dyeing, and pharmaceutical compounds. Cashew stems also yield gum that can be used in bookbinding, and the tree sap and resin have many uses.

Pistachio

Botanical name
Pistacia vera L.
Common name
pistachio

Origin and native distribution
Eastern Mediterranean
to Southwest Asia
Parts used
seeds

Different cultivars of pistachio, top to bottom: the larger Californian,
the rounder Iranian, and the narrower and longer Turkish variety.
Taste varies, and some varieties crack open more easily than others.
Below, the nearly mature drupes investigate what lies within.

Pistachio - *Pistacia vera*

Why am I smiling? This green gap of joy
Is my happiness popping me open.
Swelling maturity ripens my mirth
That cracks up, splits its sides, and tastes freedom.

Beloved by the fair Queen of Sheba; but
Brought first, it is said, by Adam to Earth;
She claimed my privilege for royalty;
Noble teeth ranked by status, ranked by birth.

Compact seeds green with their chlorophyll light
Tell you stories of cool breezy highlands.
For nine thousand years from Middle East lands
I have spread, along with the sweet almonds.

I am a luxury, smooth as ice cream,
Sweetened with holiday, salted by sea.
In layered baklava, sticky and dense,
Bright oval gems are fragrant and crunchy.

A green constellation flung wide and far,
Scattered in handfuls on rice, salads, stew,
And baba ganoush with pomegranate;
Clear garnet seeds join mine, doubly jewelled.

The shell of the pistachio splits open like a smiling mouth when the seed kernel inside ripens and swells. It is known as *the smiling pistachio* (Middle East), *the smiling nut* (Iran) and *the happy nut* (China). Pistachios are small, up to 2.5 centimetres long, and quite expensive. When you are lucky enough to have some pistachios you too ought to be smiling at such luxury.

Moslem legend declares that Adam brought pistachios to Earth, and they are mentioned along with almonds in Genesis, the first book of the Old Testament. The Queen of Sheba is said to have claimed pistachio nuts for royalty, forbidding the common people to grow the nuts for their own enjoyment.

Pistachios and almonds have been found at ancient settlements in the Middle East that date back to around 7000 BCE. Today, Iranian and Turkish varieties are considered the most flavourful, while Californian varieties tend to be larger but less tasty. Their popularity in America grew with the arrival of immigrants in the 1880s who brought the flavours of home with them to New York.

Pistachios produce male and female flowers on separate trees; both are needed to grow nuts and the trees are pollinated by the wind. In cultivation five to eight female trees are planted for each male, or grafting is used to attach a male branch to a female tree. Pistachios are deciduous, losing their leaves in autumn and resting dormant in the winter. They can tolerate long periods of drought and poor soil as their root systems find water deep in the earth; even in harsh environments the trees can stay productive for over 100 years.

The remarkable bright green seed kernel is covered with a delicate red-mauve skin, and forms inside a bone-like white shell at the centre of a fleshy egg-shaped drupe. These drupes grow in clusters and take months to mature. The pistachio's vibrant colour comes from chlorophyll, and is especially vivid in nuts from trees grown in relatively cooler climates (this is a warm-weather plant), or when harvested early. When the nuts reach full maturity their chlorophyll content decreases and the nut fades to yellow-green. Immature nuts are roasted at low temperatures to keep their colour, so when cooking pistachios at home remember that high heat is no friend to chlorophyll.

One good reason to eat pistachios is their tryptophan content; this amino acid is the precursor of serotonin. Serotonin is a neurotransmitter that helps us feel focussed, calm, contented and emotionally stable. Low levels are connected with depression and normal levels with happiness, so pistachio's claim to be *the smiling nut* is more than skin deep. They are also a good source of vitamins, minerals and other nutrients, and they taste delicious.

The characteristic flavour of pistachios makes them a popular nut to eat raw or roasted and salted or unsalted. They are made into ice cream, halva, nougat, baklava and other baked goods. They are used in soups, salads and rice dishes, and are important in Middle Eastern, Mediterranean and Indian cuisine. They give distinctive seasoning to sausages such as mortadella, zampone and saucisson de lange. A gourmet oil can be extracted from pistachios but this is so expensive to make that it is not available commercially.

Annonaceae family

Cherimoya, soursop and sugar apple

Botanical (and common) names
Annona cherimola Mill.
(cherimoya)
Annona muricata L.
(soursop, guanábana)
Annona squamosa L.
(sugar apple)

Origin and native distribution
South America,
Central America, West Indies

Parts used
fruits

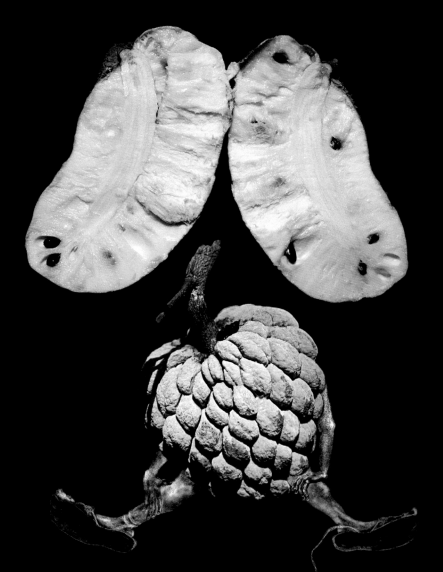

Cherimoya, soursop and sugar apple - *Annona* species

The lively green scales or warty skin texture
Of species *Annona* could well bring to mind
The protrusions of pine cones, growing in sections,
But we're plants of a totally different kind.

It's not our hard seeds that people desire,
It's the melting sweet softness under the skin.
Cherimola, muricata, squamosa: all
Create rich fruity flavours hidden within.

We prefer not to travel, so getting a taste
Could mean bringing your mouth all the way to our lands.
You'll grow warm, just like us, in the tropical sun
And can lick the ripe juice flowing over your hands.

South and Central America, and the lush Tropics;
You'll find us in lands that are fertile and hot.
For now we can give you a hint of our flavours
Until you can travel and eat up the lot.

Banana and pineapple both in one bite
Is the secret of sweet *Cherimola's* delight.

Muricata or soursop's white pulp, acid-sweet,
Has a hundred-odd seeds that you must not eat.

Sugar apple, *squamosa*, is custardy, creamy;
Once you've spooned out the seeds it's a pudding that's dreamy.

Each *Annona* above is a medicine too,
Used for years by the people who tasted them first.
Now they're studied to give us a clearer idea
Of their virtues beyond quenching hunger and thirst.

The *Annona* species all produce composite fruits resembling a scaly fir cone. The fruits are delicious with soft, sweet flesh containing many seeds. The seeds are poisonous and are used as insecticides, along with the leaves.

The fruits are native to South and Central America and are cultivated in suitably warm climates around the world. They are not widely exported as they do not travel well and are not suited to refrigeration; this makes them expensive outside their growing regions.

Cherimoya - *Annona cherimola*

The most amenable to travel of the *Annona* species, cherimoya can be harvested unripe and exported to ripen at room temperature. Under the overlapping scales of greenish or purplish colour the white flesh is fragrant, with a delicious sweet-sour banana-pineapple flavour. They are usually eaten raw, with the flesh spooned from the cut fruit, but can also be made into ice cream, sorbet, cakes, custard, yoghurt, milkshakes and wine. There are around 20 to 40 seeds in each fruit.

The cherimoya has been grown in many regions of the world since the mid-1700s. The seeds were brought to Europe where plants were grown in Spain, England and Italy. In 1785 cherimoya was taken to Jamaica and on to Haiti, and it is also found in other parts of the West Indies. In the late 1800s it was cultivated in Asia and Africa, India and Sri Lanka, and was growing in Rauol Island, New Zealand by 1887.

Soursop, guanábana - *Annona muricata*

Soursop's medicinal properties were used in the traditional remedies of the tropical Americas. Diseases such as pellagra were common among enslaved people as a result of their nutrient-poor maize-based diet, and soursop's high niacin, vitamin C and vitamin B3 content acted as a remedy. Traditional medicine in Jamaica used different parts of the plant to treat dysentery, fevers, colds and nervous conditions, all symptoms of niacin deficiency which causes pellagra. Soursop is now being researched to explore its phytochemicals and its potential as a cancer treatment.

Soursop range from ovate, heart-shaped or conical fruits with bright green skin covered with warts or short soft spines. They are the largest of the *Annona* species with an average weight of 4 kilograms. Inside the rind is white, juicy pulp with a slightly gloopy, fibrous texture. Its refreshing, sweet taste resembles pineapple and mango.

Cherimoya and sugar apple

Botanical (and common) names
Annona cherimola Mill.
(cherimoya)
Annona squamosa L.
(sugar apple)

Origin and distribution
South America,
Central America, West Indies
Parts used
fruits

Cherimoya finding out what's inside the opened sugar apple.

Throughout the flesh are found between 30 and 170 black or dark brown seeds which are toxic if consumed. The soursop can be eaten with a spoon, avoiding the seeds, or the pulp can be used for soft drinks, such as the Cuban champola de guanábana made from the strained pulp and milk. Soursop is also mixed with wine or brandy, and used as a dessert for ice cream sherbets and custards. Unripe fruits can be used in soups or fried, roasted or boiled. Young leafy shoots can be steamed and eaten as a vegetable.

Sugar apple - *Annona squamosa*

The exceptionally sweet and creamy flesh of the sugar apple makes it a popular dessert fruit. Ranging from heart-shaped, conical, rounded or ovate, it grows up to 10 centimetres in length and contains 35 to 45 black seeds. The green or reddish scaled skin has a whitish bloom. Of the few recognised cultivated varieties, India has produced the most.

Apiaceae family
Coriander

Botanical name
Coriandrum sativum L.

Common names
coriander, cilantro, dhania,
yuen sal, Chinese parsley

Origin and native distribution
Middle East, India,
Mediterranean region

Parts used
fruits, leaves, stalks, seeds, roots

Coriander fruits and fresh leaves. The larger oval fruit variety on
the left and the smaller rounded fruit variety on the right, with ground
coriander in the middle and roasted seeds at the bottom.

Coriander - *Coriandrum sativum*

I'm the most popular herb, or can claim to be.
So why do many people dislike me?
Some say I'm soapy, but others make free
With the claim "bedbug flavour" -
They say I taste "buggy"!

Now I ask you, quite seriously, how do they know?
Have they been munching their duvet,
Sucking the pillow?
"Before licking your bed
Try a curry instead",
That's surely a far better motto.

My fruits small and round blend so well with cumin,
There's hardly a curry without us two in.
You can bash up my husk to thicken the sauce,
And my green leaves are perfect for salad, of course.
Don't miss out the stalks - just chop them up thin
For your soups, stews and stir fries - throw all of me in.

Coriander or cilantro could be the world's most widely used herb, despite the scent and taste of the fresh leaves being described as "buggy", specifically "bedbug" (van Wyk), or "soapy" (McGee). Those who don't know what bedbugs taste like might describe coriander's quality as softly pungent or slightly fungi-like.

The plant's etymology shows this historical tug of war between aversion and appreciation. In Greek, its name *koriannon* is a fusion of *koris*, meaning a *stink bug*, and *annon*, a more attractively scented *anise*. The name was spelled *coriandrum* in Latin and became *coriandre* in the Old French, entering the English language in the 14th century and becoming coriander.

Coriander was one of the first spices used by humans, and was valued for its medicinal properties from ancient times. The whole plant can be eaten: leaves, stalks, flowers and roots. Traces have been found in Bronze Age ruins and in the tombs of the Pharaohs, including the resting place of Tutankhamun dating from 1325 BCE.

Coriander has developed into three main groups (morphotypes). The fruits (often wrongly called seeds) of each group have a different balance of essential oils. The most aromatic with the highest essential oil content are the small round types that have developed in the Caucasus and Central Asia. The larger round fruits with a medium to low essential oil content have come from Northern Africa, the Middle East, the Mediterranean, Europe and the New World. The Indian subcontinent has produced ovoid fruits which have a low essential oil content, but are often prized for their characteristic flavour, which is less floral than the small round types.

The mellow fragrance of dried, roasted and ground coriander is often paired with the spice cumin, forming "the coriander-cumin backbone" of Indian cooking (McGee). The fruits contain two flat seeds which, in India, are roasted and chewed as a breath freshener and eaten after meals to aid digestion. Coriander is an important ingredient in the spice blends of many nations, flavouring savoury dishes and also used in desserts and alcoholic drinks such as gin, Chartreuse and Izarra.

Fresh green coriander leaves are added to dishes at the very end of their cooking time, as the main aroma compounds quickly fade when heated. Coriander leaves and flowers can be eaten in salads, and the stringy stalks can be chopped and added to soups. The stems can also be dried and used to smoke foods, permeating them with an intense flavour. The roots of the plant are important in Thai and Chinese cooking. Their flavour is more green and woody, reminiscent of parsley; hence Chinese parsley, one of the plant's common names.

Apiaceae family
Carrot

Botanical name
Daucus carota L.

Common name
carrot

Origin and native distribution
Europe, Central Asia

Parts used
roots

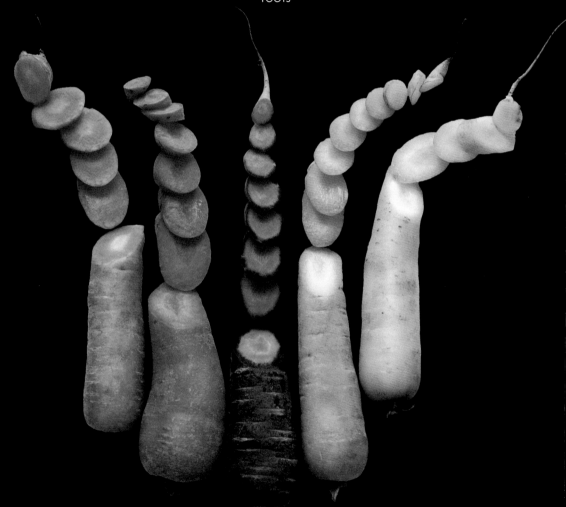

The swollen tap roots of domesticated carrots show their
colours in five cultivated varieties. These root vegetables can range
in hue from white to yellow, orange and purple.

Carrot - *Daucus carota*

I'm *Daucus carota*, you'll know me as carrot.
Have I always been orange? I tell you I have not!
In Afghanistan where I first sprang from the ground
The word of my colours soon travelled around.
I was purple or white or a warm golden hue;
Then the Dutch making history caused a to-do
By enhancing my fiery luminous glow
To praise William of Orange; there's some history you know.

Chop me up widthways and what have you found?
Little slices like pupils, perfectly round.
Pupils here means the central circles of your eyes,
Not young folks working hard in their schools for a prize,
For a carrot a day keeps the darkness at bay
As I brighten your eyes with my vitamin A,
Which helps you see far as the pale daylight fades,
Revealing night's shadows and secrets and shades.

Carotene makes things golden and this can be seen
As my extract is used to dress up margarine,
And other concoctions whose true state is pale,
To make them more beautiful when they're for sale.
Eat me raw for my goodness, I'm crunchy and sweet,
Or invite all my spicy relations to meet.
We will dive into soups and stews, ready to play:
Coriander, cumin, fennel and caraway.

Wild carrots have been gathered for thousands of years, with cultivated varieties originating in Central Asia before being distributed around the Mediterranean. Though now associated with the colour orange, the carrots first domesticated in Afghanistan were purple. They arrived in the Mediterranean in the 14th century along with white, yellow and red forms.

The Dutch are credited with developing the orange carrot in the 16th century by selecting from yellow and red varieties in honour of William I of Orange, who led the resistance during the Netherlands' war for independence from the Spanish occupation and its Inquisition. When many Dutch people fled to England they brought their orange carrots with them. The previously predominant purple and yellow varieties were thereafter neglected.

The sweetness of carrots made them historically useful for puddings and cakes when sugar or other sweeteners were expensive, such as in Europe during the Middle Ages and the Second World War. They are popular in Indian and Middle Eastern confectionery, and of course in carrot cake; they are also made into jam. Carrot leaves can be cooked as a potherb. Carrot juice is considered a health drink and is consumed raw or fermented. Carrot is an essential component of mirepoix, the blend of onion, celery and carrot which is the flavour base for French cooking and has extended to classical Western cuisine.

Recently, fresh carrots have been sold as ready-cut batons for dipping and snacking. They are protected by chemical preservatives to add up to three weeks to their shelf life, and stop them developing the white bloom that makes them look old and unpalatable. Citric acid is one of these preservatives but others are left unnamed, keeping the consumer in the dark. Carrot crops are heavily sprayed with pesticides (organic crops less so), so carrot batons potentially carry a double load of synthetic chemicals.

Carrot's vibrant colour comes from the pigment carotene, to which it gives its name as it was the first vegetable in which these chemicals were identified. The natural pigments or carotenes found in plants are often referred to as vitamin A. Strictly speaking, carotenes (of which beta-carotene is the most common) are the precursor of vitamin A. When we eat plant foods such as carrots, pumpkins, mangoes and other naturally orange foods the carotenes are converted to vitamin A by the body and stored in the liver.

Vitamin A is named retinol because it is almost identical to the retinol present in the rod cells of the retina of the human eye. These are highly sensitive and govern our ability to see at dusk and in low light.

Carrots of different colours behave differently when cooked. While the orange carrots of the West contain carotene, the Eastern carrots contain the purple-red pigment anthocyanin. Anthocyanin is water soluble so when cooked the purple colour is drawn out into the cooking liquid. To preserve their colour and nutrient content they can be enjoyed lightly sautéed. Carotene is oil and fat soluble, so orange carrots stay bright when cooked in water. Including a good quality oil in the cooking process will encourage orange carrots to release their antioxidant beta-carotene which, when converted to vitamin A, helps the eyes, builds healthy skin and cell membranes, supports the immune system, and lowers the risk of cancer.

When carotene or carrot extract is used to colour processed foods the extraction process unfortunately negates any nutritional content.

Apiaceae family
Sweet fennel and bulb fennel

Botanical name
Foeniculum vulgare Mill.

Origin and native distribution
Mediterranean region

Common names
(common fennel)
sweet fennel, fennel seeds
(azoricum variety)
Florence fennel,
finocchio, bulb fennel

Parts used
(common fennel) dry fruits
("seeds"), leaves, leaf stalks
(azoricum variety)
swollen leaf bases ("bulbs"),
leaves, seeds

A pair of Florence or bulb fennel holding the small
but potent sweet fennel seeds

Sweet fennel (common fennel) - *Foeniculum vulgare*

What's that rumbling sound? Is that your digestion?
Goodness me - in that case may I make a suggestion?
Be Indian - crunch up my seeds after eating
So flatulence won't send your best friends retreating.
Sweet fennel gives fruits and leaves small but so strong,
We're your friend when digestion has gone a bit wrong.
I've a bold taste of aniseed - don't use too much
Even if your poor tummy's too swollen to touch.
I will sweeten your breath and spice up your stew,
Make tisane, soothe your tum, and take good care of you.

Bulb fennel (azoricum variety) - *Foeniculum vulgare*

Like my sibling sweet fennel I'm one of the plants
Raised up by the bright Mediterranean sun.
Florence fennel I'm known within Italy's borders,
And through the cuisine of the warm South I run.
My clear anise aroma, my swell and my crunch
Can be softened with baking. But sliced and kept raw
And sprinkled with orange juice, oil, nuts and seeds
I'll create a fresh salad that all will adore.

When the Greeks won victory over the Persians at the Battle of Marathon in 490 BCE they did so fighting in a field of fennel, *marathos* or *marathon*. This plant gave its name to the place and to the long run by which the herald brought the news of success to Athens. What we call fennel seeds are actually fruits. Everyday language is not always botanically accurate so most people speak of fennel seeds.

The medical use of sweet fennel dates from around the 13th century BCE during the Mycenaean civilisation. Fennel seeds are carminative (relieving flatulence and bloating) and they improve digestion; a tisane can be made by steeping the seeds or leaves in hot water. In India, sugar-coated fennel seeds are eaten after meals to aid digestion and sweeten the breath. A teaspoon of cooled weak fennel tisane can be used as gripe water for infants with colic. More recently a series of studies has shown that sweet fennel is effective in controlling infectious disorders of bacterial, fungal, viral, and protozoan origin.

The flavour of fennel pairs well with its family members carrots and caraway. A dish of carrots cooked with fennel, caraway and perhaps a pinch of dried red chilli flakes is very flavoursome, and the addition of red lentils can make a hearty spiced soup.

Fennel's thin feathery leaves are used as a garnish and a seasoning, and in Champsac mustard. They are often used with fish. The stems and flower heads can be eaten as vegetables. Even the fine yellow pollen from the flowers can be used as a spice combining a floral delicacy with fennel's anise aroma; it is traditionally used in Italy, sprinkled over soups, stews and other dishes just before serving. Fennel oil is widely used for flavouring liqueurs such as Sambuca, Absinthe and Pernod. It is also used as a complement to the dominant flavour of star anise in Anisette, Ouzo, Pastis and Raki.

Azoricum variety or bulb fennel is a smaller plant than common fennel. It is a different cultivated variety of the same species, and the bulb-like leafstalks base is eaten. The common name Florence fennel comes from its importance in Italy and Sicily where it is known as *carosella*.

Bulb fennel is eaten raw in salads or cooked, often baked in a creamy sauce. The leaves can be used fresh or dried. Raw bulb fennel is high in calcium. To make a simple salad, finely slice a fennel bulb and spread the layers out in a dish. Drench the fennel in a dressing made from freshly squeezed orange juice, olive oil, salt and pepper, and sprinkle over sunflower seeds or chopped toasted hazelnuts.

Hamburg parsley – Tuberosum group

Botanical name
Petroselinum crispum (Mill.) Fuss

Common names
Hamburg parsley,
parsnip-rooted parsley,
German parsley

Origin and native distribution
Mediterranean region, Sardinia

Parts used
roots, leaves

What's in the dish? The fleshy, tapering roots of Hamburg or parsnip-rooted
parsley are often made into hearty stews,

Hamburg parsley - *Petroselinum crispum*

I may not look like much.
Not bright like a carrot.
Not broad like a parsnip.
Not shouting my wares to the crowd.
But in this slim root
And in my green leaves
There is flavour.
Try my taste.
Raw or roasted,
Mashed or chipped,
Grated or smothered
In sauce - you'll see.
Germany, Poland,
And Russia all know me.
So shall we meet?

The fleshy, somewhat twisting roots of Hamburg parsley are popular in northern Germany, Eastern Europe, Russia and the Netherlands, but are generally overlooked throughout much of Europe. They are a tasty and versatile if unattractive vegetable. Their flavour has been likened to a more delicate parsnip or a nutty combination of celery and parsley. They are often referred to as parsley root.

Hamburg parsley possesses the classic root vegetable's firmness of texture, making it useful in hearty soups and stews such as borsch and as an alternative to potatoes for frying, roasting, mashing, or making chips. The roots are thin-skinned enough to require no peeling. Once washed, and after any stray hairs or tendrils have been gently shaved off, they can be cooked to tenderness but not beyond in order to preserve their flavour. The vegetable can be eaten raw, and the young leaves can be cooked as a potherb.

To prevent the roots discolouring during preparation, lemon juice can be squeezed over its flesh or it can be cut directly into a pan of water with a dash of lemon juice added.

Apiaceae family
Parsley

Botanical name
Petroselinum crispum (Mill.) Fuss

Common names
parsley, curly-leaf parsley,
flat-leaf parsley

Origin and native distribution
Mediterranean region

Parts used
leaves

Cultivated Italian flat-leaved parsley (also known as celery-leaved parsley),
and the common variety of parsley with crisped or curly leaves.

Parsley - *Petroselinum crispum*

I'm *Petroselinum crispum*, or *rock celery*
If you want to translate ancient Greek.
You've probably noticed that old names tell tales
And of family history speak.
The Romans of old, now they loved a good bath,
It was something they hated to miss.
They chewed parsley, as cleanliness comes from within;
Garlic breath will not win you a kiss.
The Greeks hardly ate me; instead they would wear me
As laurels and crowns of bright green,
Proof of victory true; and like Romans they knew
That I'd keep a fresh corpse smelling clean.
Although I'm so lively in flavour and colour,
With iron and vitamin C,
For these civilisations when someone was dying
The call went up, "bring the parsley!"

But all that's behind me: today I am very much
Part of the modern chef's game.
In tabbouleh, soup, salad, sauces for fish,
And as medicine I've found my fame.
I have calcium in me, that helps bones grow strong
So your skeleton stands nice and straight.
I'm much more than a garnish, and you could do worse
Than have handfuls of me on your plate.
Before death arrives (as it will for us all
In the end, so there's no need to fear)
Try my leaves flat or curly, gather your friends,
And enjoy me now, while you're still here.

Parsley is an ancient cure-all, valued for its cleansing and medicinal properties. The ancient Greeks and Romans relied on it as a purifier of bad smells. It was chewed to mask garlic seeping out on the breath and in sweat, and was used in the preparation of dead bodies to keep them smelling fresh before burial. For hundreds of years, parsley was used by these cultures more for its medicinal and spiritual potency than as a food.

Parsley's place in Greek funeral rites gave it sanctity as well as everyday usefulness. It was worn as laurels or wreaths around the head not only by funeral mourners but by victorious athletes at sporting competitions. In the Hebrew tradition parsley was also significant, as it represented rebirth in the spring festival of Passover.

Eventually, around the Middle Ages, parsley gained popularity as a flavourful and nutritious herb. It can be used as a main ingredient as well as a garnish. Its dark green leaves, whether curly or flat, are full of iron and calcium, and benefit the gut microbiome.

The Middle Eastern dish tabbouleh uses great quantities of fresh parsley in a salad with bulgur wheat, tomatoes, mint and other lively flavours, and it often features in ful medames, a warm dish made with brown broad beans. Parsley can be used as the primary flavour in soups and sauces, and is popular in a white sauce for fish. It is a common addition to salads, stuffings and omelettes. Parsley is also used as a dried herb, and an oil extracted from the seeds and leaves is used in the food industry.

There are three varieties of parsley: the curly- (*Petroselinum crispum* var. *crispum*) and flat-leaved (*Petroselinum crispum* var. *neapolitanum*) where the greens are eaten, and the Hamburg parsley (*Petroselinum crispum* var. *tuberosum*) which is cultivated for its edible tubers.

Araucariaceae family
Paraná pine

Botanical name
Araucaria angustifolia (Bertol.) Kuntze

Common name
Paraná pine,
Brazilian pine,
candelabra tree

Origin and native distribution
Southern Brazil,
Northeast Argentina, Paraguay

Parts used
seeds

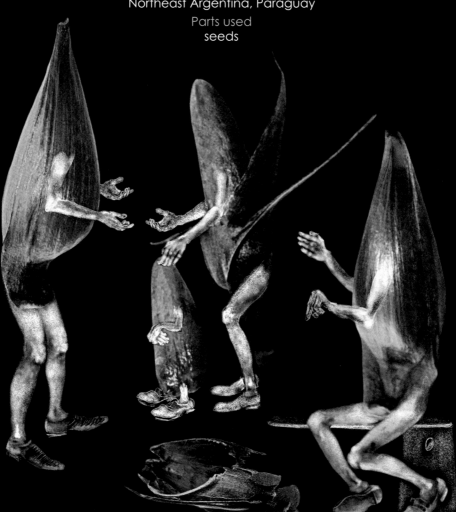

The nut-like seeds in their bright brown protective coat can grow to around
5 centimetres long, and the seed kernels are a popular winter snack.

Araucariaceae family

Paraná pine - *Araucaria angustifolia*

This popular pine has an uncertain future.
Affection and appetite are rivals in life.
One keeps me growing, cares for my homeland;
The other takes greedily, leaves tomorrow to chance.

In one hundred years I've lost most of my trees.
The forests I filled are now thinning too fast.
And what of the mammals and birds who rely
On my seeds in the winter, to keep them alive?

So give me some time and some space to recover;
Leave me to birds and to beasts for a while.
I can meet some demands but I balk at destruction.
Please solve this puzzle before too much time passes.

Over the past 100 years, numbers of Paraná pine have crashed by 97% in its native Brazil, Argentina and Paraguay, and it is currently assessed as Critically Endangered. Its future is at risk as forests are cut down for timber, and seeds are intensively harvested without leaving enough seeds behind for regeneration of the species and the ecosystems it nurtures.

After pollination, the Paraná pine seed cones take three to four years to mature. The seeds only remain viable for a few weeks and are quick to germinate once they have fallen from the tree. The large cones measure 18 to 25 centimetres and each holds around 100 to 150 seeds of 5 centimetres in length. Once mature, the cone falls apart to release the seeds, which are eaten by birds and mammals including domestic pigs and peccaries. The azure jay plays an important role in dispersing the seeds.

In southern Brazil the seeds, called pinhão, are an important traditional food for indigenous Americans and they are also used in folk medicine. Although the indigenous population is small, over 3,000 tons of seeds are collected each year as a result of their popularity throughout the country. There is a pinhão fair held in the Brazilian city of Lages at which boiled seeds are eaten with hot wine.

The highly nutritious seeds are cooked and hulled before being eaten, and the flavour is similar to that of sweet potatoes. The seeds can be made into a flour used in regional dishes. The tree also produces an edible gum.

In the UK the species is adapting well to a climate radically different to that of its native lands, within the Bedgebury National Pinetum in Kent, a globally important centre for species conservation and the study of conifers. Paraná pine is a close relative of the monkey puzzle tree (*Araucaria araucana*).

Date

Botanical name
Phoenix dactylifera L.

Common name
date palm

Origin and native distribution
Middle Eastern and African oases

Parts used
ripe fruits

Date fruits at three different stages of maturation, all edible:
mature but unripe yellow *Khalal* or *Bisr* (50% moisture), ripened *Rutab*
(30% to 35% moisture), and mature *Tamr* (10% to 30% moisture).
The reddish fruits in the centre are Chinese dates or jujubes, which
are not related to the date palm. They have a dry, spongy texture
and a similar taste to dates, though not quite as sweet.

Date - *Phoenix dactylifera*

How will we find the rare oases,
Those heartbeats dropped into desert silence?
I will show you, I will guide you.
How will we find the strength to journey there,
With bodies so weary and mouths so dry?
I will nourish you, I will strengthen you.
How will we shelter from wind and sun,
The sand flung into our eyes and noses?
I will cover you, I will build for you.

Ancient I was when Palmyra was shaped,
Trusted and chosen by each generation.
Treasured by humans, who carved me at Nineveh,
Who honoured the Moon God of Ur with my wood.
Temples and cultures I've raised with my body,
My fruits in their clusters establishing trade.

Phoenix dactylifera, Greek for *red fingers*,
One of the first five trees bearing fruit
To be taken to heart and carried through history.
Date, olive, grapevine, fig, pomegranate,
Lush ripe lifeblood that raised humankind
And sustains to this day its pleasures and journeys,
Blessing each hopeful step, our paths intertwined.

The date palm has always been a welcome sight in the desert, a reliable sign of an oasis and sustenance. As the Arab proverb says "its feet shall be in a stream of water, and its head in the furnace of heaven". Thriving in hot, dry climates with little rain by absorbing underground moisture through its roots, the palm tells travellers that ground water is near and to look hopefully for wadis and ravines.

Phoenix dactylifera is a palm in the same family as the coconut and oil palms. While bats, birds and the wind have played their part, it was humans who were responsible for the wide dispersal of dates. Among the early palm cultivators were the Phoenicians, great travellers who spread the popularity of date palms along their trade routes. Dates are perfectly suited to long journeys; easily portable, high in sugars and low in moisture so they keep well and are an energy-rich food. Dates are also full of nutrients that help build healthy body tissue and muscle, including vitamin A and B-complex vitamins.

Dates have been cultivated since at least 4000 BCE and the tree's trunk, leaves and fibres have many practical uses, so the date naturally gained great cultural significance. The Assyrians of Mesopotamia used date wood in the construction of the great Ziggurat (temple) of the Moon god Ur around 2100 BCE, and date palms were carved in bas-reliefs at their capital Nineveh (such as the Assyrian bas-relief now in the British Museum). Seeds 5,000 years old were found in the ruins of the ancient Indus city Mohenjo Daro in the Sindh province of Pakistan. At the ancient oasis city in the heart of the Syrian desert the abundance of palms was echoed in its name, Palmyra. When the Abrahamic religions arose in Israel, a date-cultivating region, the fruits found their way into the sacred texts and practices of Judaism, Christianity and Islam. The date is mentioned more often than any other fruit in the Qur'an, and during the month of Ramadan Muslims will traditionally break their fast by eating a date before the evening meal.

Dates can be bought in many guises, from dried to a state of near-mummification to soft and oozing with sticky juice. The soft, melting flesh of varieties like Medjool and Deglet Nour is best enjoyed simply. A bath of cardamom-spiced coffee; a splash of orange blossom water; the crunch of a few nuts and a serving of yoghurt; any combination of these creates a delicious dish that lets the date's qualities shine.

The Chinese date or jujube, *Ziziphus jujuba*, is not related to the date palm despite its similarity in appearance and culinary use. It belongs to the buckthorn family (*Rhamnaceae*), and its history of cultivation in China goes back at least 4,000 years. It is very high in vitamin C.

Arecaceae family
Snake fruit

Botanical name
Salacca zalacca (Gaertn.) Voss
Common names
snake fruit, salak
Origin and native distribution
Southeast Asia
Parts used
ripe and unripe fruits

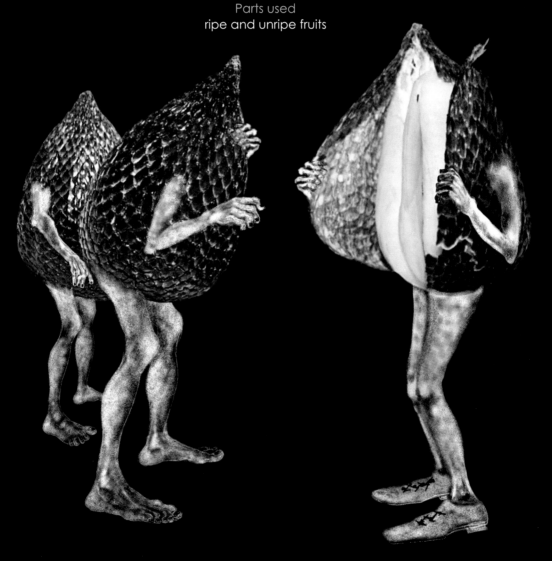

A partially opened snake fruit showing its whole companions
what's inside the shiny jacket: hard, pale yellow pulp that breaks apart
into three lobes, which resemble large cloves of garlic.

Snake fruit - *Salacca zalacca*

What is encased in this smooth snakeskin jacket,
This teardrop of shining brown scales pulled so tight?
Firm honeyed segments of flesh, yellow-white crispness,
Each hugs the fine glossy seed that it holds.

Salacca zalacca sounds like a spell,
An abracadabra to conjure desire.
I am salak, snake fruit, sweet antioxidant.
Tropical Asia is where I call home.

Seek at the heart of the female palms
If you dare the sharp spines that bar your way.
Among leaves flowing up from the warm scented earth
You'll find me close to the ground, lying low.

Snake fruit or salak, its Malaysian name, is considered one of the tastiest palm fruits for eating fresh from the tree.

It is important to the economy of its growing regions, being cultivated for home kitchen use and for sale in local and international markets. It is a popular garden fencing plant as in addition to providing fruit, when planted close together the spiny palms deter intruders. The bark of the petioles (leaf stalks) is also used for matting and the leaflets for thatching. Due to the extremely spiny leaves the fruits require careful harvesting.

Unusually for a palm or tree fruit, which we most often find hanging from high branches, snake fruit grow in clusters at the base of the tree. The leaves also grow from this almost trunkless base, rather than as a canopy. The leaves can reach up to 10 metres long and the trees can be fruitful for around 50 years. Male and female flowers grow on separate trees, and only the female trees bear fruits. The tree also produces edible palm hearts.

Snake fruit is most commonly eaten fresh or as juice, but unripe fruits can be preserved or cooked with spices. The fruit is very nutritious and high in antioxidants. It is a subject of pharmacological studies; analysis of the flesh and peel show its medicinal potential as an anti-inflammatory, anti-cancer and anti-diabetic agent.

Asparagus

Botanical name
Asparagus officinalis L.

Common name
asparagus

Origin and native distribution
North Africa, Central and Southern Europe,
Western and Central Asia

Parts used
young stems ("spears")

Top, left to right: unopened flower shoots of *Ornithogalum pyrenaicum* next
to its close relative, common green asparagus.
Bottom: white asparagus, pale from lack of sunlight.

Asparagus - *Asparagus officinalis*

Yes, I remember the times that have passed.
I recall the Egyptians,
The gleam of gold-flecked lapis lazuli
On brown necks scented with myrrh.
The Romans linger in memory,
Those long epicurean meals where the wine
Never ceased flowing, like time itself.
Their mirth echoing around frescoed walls
As they spoke of my shape and the night ahead.
Slaves treading softly in the shadows.
My spears upright and firm are vigorous and cherished,
Cut down by hand as spring ripens to summer.
In my memory I am always so young and prized.
Youth's tenderness needs only a little attention
To reach its perfection, to furnish the feast.
Gentle steam, a hot bath, or charred just a touch.
No more adornment than oil, melting gold.
My influence lingers beyond the meal.
I follow the diners home,
Each recalling my presence long into the scented night.

Asparagus is a demanding and expensive vegetable to grow, requiring vigilance and hand-picking. It has a short season from late spring to early summer, and only the young shoots or "spears" should be eaten. Once the tip breaks through the soil and into the light it can grow between 12 to 25 centimetres in one day, and it is this day-old growth which is harvested. These spears are tender, crunchy and bitter-sweet.

There are around 150 species of asparagus native to North Africa, Europe and east into Siberia. The most important cultivated species, *Asparagus officinalis*, is also the most important wild species; their seeds are spread by birds.

Asparagus can be green, white, or purple. All wild asparagus is green, but botanically green and white asparagus are the same. To grow white asparagus the roots are planted deeper in the soil, away from the sunlight. This prevents photosynthesis, sunlight's stimulation of the plant's production of green chlorophyll. Harvested as soon as the tip breaks the soil, white asparagus has a more delicate flavour.

Purple asparagus was developed near the city of Albenga in Italy, hence the cultivar's name *Violettto d'Albenga*. It contains more sugar and less fibre than the green and white varieties, and its purple colour comes from anthocyanins which give the red-purple colour to other food plants.

The cultivation of asparagus for food dates back to the ancient Egyptians, and it was valued by those Romans who could afford it. It was also prized for its medicinal use by many cultures, such as those in China and Africa. The plant is rich in vitamins A, C and E, and acts as a diuretic. As well as encouraging the production of urine it can give it a strong odour, but not everyone produces it or can smell it. The after-effects of asparagus and your detection of them depends on your genetics.

Asparagus benefits from quick, simple cooking to highlight its texture and flavour. It can be briefly boiled or chargrilled so it doesn't become droopy. It is often eaten whole with the hands, dipped into a simple sauce of melted butter or vinaigrette (olive oil and lemon juice). It can also be sliced and added to stir-fries and risottos, and the lower, tougher part of the spears can be added to soups.

Similar to asparagus, and belonging to the same family, is *Ornithogalum pyrenaicum*, also called Prussian asparagus, Bath asparagus, Pyrenees star of Bethlehem or spiked star of Bethlehem. This plant is a wild flower whose unopened flower shoots can be eaten in the same way as asparagus. It is native to the UK, Europe and North Africa.

Asparagaceae family

Asparagus

Botanical name
Asparagus officinalis L.
Common name
asparagus

Origin and native distribution
North Africa, Central
and Southern Europe,
Western and Central Asia
Parts used
young stems ("spears")

Purple asparagus bringing butter for a simple sauce.
Originally developed in Italy, purple asparagus has higher sugar
and lower fibre levels than green and white varieties.

Globe artichoke

Botanical name	Origin and native distribution
Cynara scolymus L.	Mediterranean region
Common names	Parts used
globe artichoke, edible thistle	immature flower heads

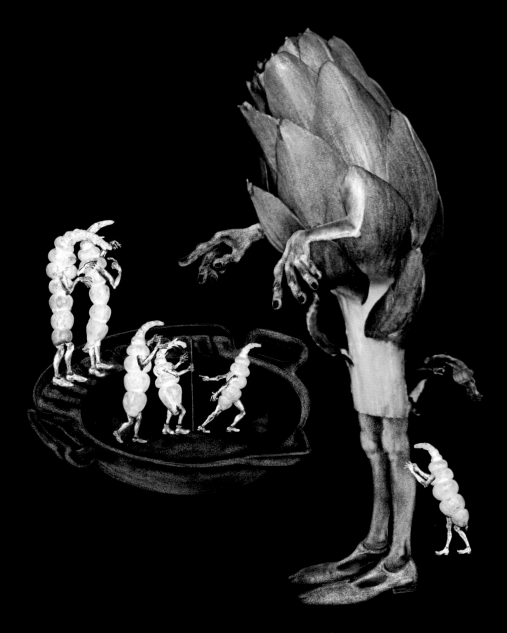

Despite being from the unrelated mint family *Lamiaceae*,
Chinese artichokes are appealing for inclusion to the globe artichoke
from the sunflower family *Asteraceae*.

Globe artichoke - *Cynara scolymus*

Have you ever put a thistle in your mouth?
Or eaten flowers before they've had a chance to bloom?
Cauliflower, broccoli, these are flowers so now try me,
You'll find me in the Mediterranean South.

My bud is picked for you while closed and tight.
Still young, my scaly bracts and tender bases
With my fond or fleshy heart, these most treasured, tasty parts
Are munched before my purple flower sees the light.

The Greeks and Romans ate me year after year.
The amorous King Henry VIII sought out my taste.
Catherine de Medici had too much appetite for me
And I rewarded her greed with the diarrhoea.

I will not harm you if you treat me with some skill.
Raw with a dressing, boiled, deep fried or bathed in oil.
Pizza, pasta, salad, stew can all make room for thistles too,
So don't eat fields of me and I won't make you ill.

The globe artichoke is native to the Mediterranean and thrives in warm climates, but some cultivated varieties have been bred to tolerate cooler temperatures. This has expanded the growing region to countries further north.

The plant is a kind of thistle, plants distinguished by the sharp prickles on their leaves and sometimes on their stems as well. Two other edible species are also referred to as artichokes, the Chinese artichoke (*Stachys affinis*, from the mint family) and the Jerusalem artichoke (*Helianthus tuberosus*, from the same sunflower family as the globe artichoke). Unlike the globe artichoke where the flower head is eaten, these two are cultivated for their tuberous roots.

The globe artichoke flower blooms purple, and grows on a stem up to 2 metres tall, with long silvery-green spiky leaves. The flower bud is around 10 to 15 centimetres wide and is formed of distinctive triangular scales or "bracts". The bases of these scales are soft, fleshy and edible, and the very base of the flower bud, called the "heart", is also eaten. At the centre of the flower bud is the "choke", an inedible, hairy mass. The stems of artichokes are also edible, but they are often overlooked.

The flavour of artichoke heart and stem is slightly sweet and delicately nutty, while the bracts are mild and creamy. Artichokes provide a good amount of iron and potassium. The leaves and stems are used medicinally for their cynarin content. This chemical encourages the liver to produce bile, an important liquid which helps in the digestion of fats.

The ancient Greeks and Romans were fond of the globe artichoke, and it gradually spread throughout Europe. Catherine de Medici is credited with bringing the vegetable to France, but as well as popularising it she served as a warning of its powers. She is recorded as suffering from terrible diarrhoea when her fondness for artichoke hearts led her to overindulge. England was introduced to artichokes by the Dutch, and they were grown on the estate at Henry VIII's Essex country house Beaulieu (New Hall).

The whole artichoke flower bud can be boiled or steamed, and the scales or bracts peeled off and eaten dipped in a sauce of butter, vinegar, mayonnaise or other dressings. Artichoke hearts are preserved by marinating them in oil for use in salads and other dishes. In Italy they are the spring vegetable on Four Seasons pizzas, and artichokes flavour Cynar liqueur. They are widely used in Spain and in Greece, which provides the artichoke origin story. A Greek myths tells the story of Cynara, a young woman who had the misfortune to attract the notice of Zeus. The father of the gods had a habit of transforming himself and his amours, and it was Cynara's fate to become the first artichoke.

Asteraceae family

Jerusalem artichoke and Chinese artichoke

Botanical name
Helianthus tuberosus L.

Common names
Jerusalem artichoke,
sunroof, sunchoke

Origin and native distribution
North America

Parts used
rhizomes

Botanical name
Stachys affinis Bunge

Family: *Lamiaceae*

Common names
Chinese artichoke, Japanese
artichoke, crosne

Origin and native distribution
East Asia

Parts used
rhizomes

Jerusalem artichokes from the *Asteraceae* family confirming that
Chinese artichokes belong to the *Lamiaceae* (mint) family.

Jerusalem artichoke and Chinese artichoke
- Helianthus tuberosus and *Stachys affinis*

Like many before I've been misunderstood,
Named for plants and lands far from my clan.
Let's set things out clearly now, I will feel good
Knowing you've made time to understand.

Girasole means *sunflower* in Italian;
I'm the American plant's rhizome,
Misheard by the British as Jerusalem
As the traders found me a new home.

Now artichoke, that was the taste that came to
The sailors who tried to describe me.
For five hundred years I've been waiting for you
To unearth the story inside me.

Here's *Stachys affinis*, whose string of jade beads
Tempts the eye but confuses the knife.
So fiddly to peel, Chinese artichoke needs
Explanation: confusion is rife!

It's not my relation, it's from the mint clan
And grows in the warm earth of Asia.
But names, as you know, rarely follow a plan;
So focus on taste, on pure pleasure.

Jerusalem artichoke - *Helianthus tuberosus*

Jerusalem artichokes are the tuberous roots of a type of North American sunflower. The plant produces clusters of yellow flowers, smaller than the classic single-headed sunflower. The lumpy tubers can be yellow, white or red and were cultivated by the Native Americans, entering European diets in the 16th century.

One explanation for the plant's common name is that when different European nationalities settled in America, the British misheard the Italian pronunciation of *girasole*, sunflower, as *Jerusalem*. The tuber's texture and taste reminded the Europeans of the globe artichokes of the Mediterranean, and it is part of the same family. Its other common name is sunchoke.

Jerusalem artichokes have a reputation for causing flatulence (they are nicknamed "fartichokes"), an unfortunate side effect of one of their beneficial properties. The starchy texture of the tubers is due not to starch carbohydrates but to fructans. These are non-digestible carbohydrates, mainly inulin fibres, which function as helpful prebiotics. While humans cannot digest these plant fibres, our gut bacteria can, so eating Jerusalem artichokes promotes the growth of beneficial bacteria in the microbiome. This makes your digestive system work better, but the bacteria generate gases as they feed, leading to the tuber's windy results.

Inulin has a high fructose content, which is not broken down into simple sugars like other carbohydrates. As they do not raise blood sugar levels, Jerusalem artichokes can be a good food for diabetics, and they also contain plenty of phosphorous and potassium. Their irregular knobbly shape makes them fiddly to peel, and they are not widely grown for food. They are mostly cultivated for use in the bioethanol, food and pharmaceutical industries. Inulin extracted from the tubers is used in medicines, nutritional supplements and to fortify other foods.

To enjoy the benefits of the vegetable without the gassy encore, they can be lacto-fermented just as cabbage is to make sauerkraut. As the finely sliced and salted tuber ferments, bacteria will be consuming the inulin and releasing their gases in the jar before they enter the body, resulting in a more digestible delicacy. This also preserves the many nutritional benefits we gain from eating the whole vegetable, such as proteins and amino acids, rather than an industrially extracted component. The tubers can be eaten like potatoes, and they are also suitable for eating raw. They can be sliced or chopped into salads, boiled, baked, fried, and pickled, as well as used in pies, soups and stews.

Chinese artichoke - *Stachys affinis*

The Chinese or Japanese artichoke is an East Asian member of the mint (*Lamiaceae*) family, whose common name comes from its similarity to globe artichoke in flavour, but definitely not in appearance. Its other common name, crosne, comes from the garden in France where it was introduced from China in the 19th century. The tuber is used in much the same way as Jerusalem artichokes; as a crisp, starchy vegetable with a pleasing nutty sweetness.

Despite not being related to Jerusalem artichokes, they share a common side effect: they can make the consumer gassy when eaten in large quantities. In the case of Chinese artichokes this is due to their indigestible stachyose carbohydrate.

The distinctive shape of the tubers, like a short length of pale globes joined together, led to their poetic description as jade beads. Jade is a sacred and valued precious stone in China, so this is high praise. Their translucent whiteness fades quickly when their flesh meets the air as, like some potatoes, they can discolour quickly once peeled. They can also lose their flavour, so to preserve their fine qualities they should be prepared quickly and not overcooked. Their bobbly shape makes them difficult to peel, so although they are easy to grow they are not a big commercial crop outside Asia.

They can be eaten with minimal preparation: washed rather than peeled, and sautéed in butter or cooked with just a little water, some butter or oil, and a pinch of salt. They can be served in their cooking liquor or with a light vinaigrette, as the aim is to taste the vegetable rather than any additional trimmings. They can also be pickled like umeboshi plums, and this is a popular delicacy in Japan.

Asteraceae family
Sunflower seed

Botanical name
Helianthus annuus L.
Common name
sunflower seeds
Origin and native distribution
North America
Parts used
seeds

Sunflower seeds in their variety, with husked seeds at the top.
The small black seeds are mainly used to produce oil, and the larger,
striped seeds are popular for eating.

Sunflower seed - *Helianthus annuus*

A tall proud American, standing and smiling,
My abundance is shared with the world at my feet.
A friend to all creatures feathered and flying,
Creeping or walking on four legs or two.
Sturdy stem, hairy leaves, strong enough to bear stroking,
Petals of gold round a dark centre full;
Bursting with seeds to feed birds, beasts and men.

The prizes I win are for more than just beauty:
My golden oil flows out over the globe,
My seeds scatter freely and fields are sun-filled.
Beyond all my virtues, statistics and facts
I'm a sight that gives joy wherever I'm seen.
Even Van Gogh's gloom lifted while painting his *Sunflowers*,
Their petals curling and lighting the room.

In my seed-patterned face you can read a great mystery,
The universal patterns, Fibonacci's truth
That harmonious spirals occur throughout nature:
In the depths of the oceans, in the hearts of gold flowers,
In a snail's brittle shell and more still undiscovered.
When life seems chaotic or empty of meaning,
Lean your mind on my strong, bright, and upstanding proof.

North America is not known for its native food crops, but the sunflower *Helianthus annuus* was domesticated around 4,000 years ago and was an important plant for the Native Americans. The seeds provided energy-rich food, and the flowers were included in ceremonial dances. The plant was also used as a medicine, and blue and red dyes were made from the seed husks. The South American Inca also valued the sunflower, and it symbolised their sun god.

Now, in summer, there are fields of these towering golden-yellow flowers across Europe, spreading on into Russia and China. The botanical name *Helianthus* combines two Greek words and means *flower of the sun* while *annuus* is from the Latin meaning *annual*. The flower heads turn to follow the sun's progress throughout the day. The plants can grow up to five metres tall and the beautiful flower head can sometimes measure half a metre in diameter.

Sunflower seeds grow with mathematical precision within their rim of bright petals. They are an example of the Fibonacci sequence, a harmonious spiral observed throughout nature. They were the subject of one of Vincent Van Gogh's most famous paintings, one of the world's most popular images.

Two types of sunflower seeds are grown, with many variations of size and shape. The type mainly grown for its oil content is small and black, which yields the sunflower oil used in cooking, dressings, margarine and spreads. Some Russian cultivars yield half their weight in oil as a result of selection and development. The type mainly eaten as a snack or used in cooking is the larger type, often with black-and-white-striped husks.

The seeds and their oil are high in the linoleic acid we need to keep cell membranes strong and supple, so they benefit the whole body on a cellular level. They also contain phenolic antioxidants that support the immune system, and plenty of protein and amino acids. As with all oil-rich seeds they should be stored away from heat and light, and eaten as fresh as possible, as they can quickly become rancid. Sunflower seed oil is more rich in vitamin E than other vegetable oils, but because of its high fat content it is best used in moderation.

Seeds are eaten raw, roasted, salted, processed into nut butter or ground into flour. They are widely used in baking and confectionery, sprinkled over salads, and used in granola and cereals. Sunflower petals can also be cooked and eaten, and the young seedlings can be used in salads. It is not just humans who benefit from sunflower seeds; they are eaten by birds, and the seed cake which is left after the oil has been extracted can be fed to livestock.

Betulaceae family

Hazelnut

Botanical name
Corylus avellana L.

Common names
hazelnut, cobnut, filbert

Origin and native distribution
Europe, Central Asia

Parts used
seeds

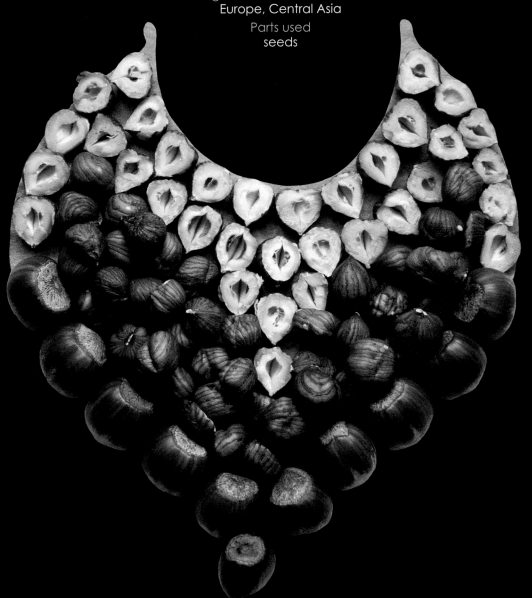

Shelled hazelnuts surrounded by larger, unshelled nuts. Cultivars vary in size,
shape and taste; their flavour and aroma is enhanced by roasting.

Hazelnut - *Corylus avellana*

The Salmon

I fed the Salmon of Knowledge of old,
Dropping hazelnuts into dark waters.
Nine trees and nine nuts.
All the wisdom on earth.
Through air into water they fell to be swallowed.
So I opened the great Salmon's mind to the path,
To the journey, the finding, the leaping to future.
The most kenning creature, he taught all his sons
And his daughters to seek the sea; seek out life.

The Squirrel

Who unleashed these ghost jumpers, tail twitchers, branch shudderers,
Squeak barkers, staccato-shout open-mouthed tooth barers?
Stripping my harvest before humans have woken,
Leaving broken shells sharp underfoot; empty tokens
Of triumph, and more sacred territory gone.
Not like the red shadows who've fled to the North.
They were smaller, and softer; a gentler touch.
Canny grey scrabblers and grabbers are fat
With their cleverness, but deeper wisdom they lack.
Leaving others' mouths empty is not the old way.
Come back, my red squirrels.
Come back and stay.

The Supermarket

I'm enthroned and enrobed in chocolate now,
Nestled in foil of gold, royal purple.
Selected and roasted, kept whole or chopped
With the finest ingredients - and fat.
Soft flour and sugar, cocoa and cream,
Liqueurs and syrups of sweet clarity,
Or in dukkah I'm spiced and savoury.
To entice my sweetness, light up the fires;
I'll release my aroma and your desire.
Yet there's wisdom still in simplicity.
Anchor your mind and remember well
That nine hazelnuts, neither salted nor sweet,
Taught a fish to be free of the world's tight net.

Hazelnuts are steeped in magic in Britain and Ireland, where they are a common hedgerow and woodland tree. Their wood is traditionally used for dowsing rods and magic wands. The Irish myth of the Salmon of Knowledge tells how the nine hazel trees surrounding Connla's Well each dropped a nut into the water, where a salmon swallowed them and gained all knowledge. This is often interpreted as the source of the salmon's ability to navigate on its long migratory journeys between their birth rivers and the sea (recent studies show that they use the earth's magnetic field).

Hazel trees grow throughout Europe and Central Asia, and their seeds have been part of the human diet since prehistoric times. They are high in energy, providing fat, vitamin E, amino acids and minerals. Hazelnuts are delicious raw or cooked, and their aroma and flavour are enhanced by roasting. They can be eaten both as the ripe brown-shelled nut, and when young and green-shelled. These young nuts, often called cobnuts in Britain and Ireland, are pale, creamy and tender. The most common cultivated variety eaten green is the Kent cobnut. Roughway Farm in Kent houses a national collection of cobnut varieties.

The nuts are named mostly for the fine, leafy husk that clings to their base. As the nuts hang in clusters, their husks appear like caps, wigs, or beards, depending on which way you look. *Corylus* comes from the Greek *korys*, meaning *hood* or *helmet*. The Anglo-Saxon *haesil* means a *head dress*. Filbert could refer either to a *full beard*, or to St Philbert's Day on 20 August, the month when the nuts ripen and fall from their leafy decoration (if grey squirrels haven't munched through the whole harvest when still green). The names also refer to the shapes of different species. Historically, when the husk is shorter than the nut it is called a *hazel*, when the husk and nut are the same length it's a *cob*, and when the nut is shorter than the husk it's a *filbert*.

Hazelnut is often paired with chocolate. The nuts are widely used in baking and confectionery, and to flavour the liqueur Frangelico. The nut's savoury uses include dukkah, an Egyptian spice blend. They are also used in Spanish and Catalonian sauces such as picada and romesco. The young, broad leaves are used as food wrappers in Turkey. The Piedmont region of Italy is famous for its hazelnuts, and they were traditionally an important crop in Southern England, where some ancient varieties still grow.

Hazel trees are often coppiced to give shoots that are strong and pliable. These are used for fishing rods, making baskets, wattle and daub houses, walking sticks, fencing hurdles, poles for growing legumes, and firewood.

Lipstick tree

Botanical name
Bixa orellana L.

Common names
lipstick tree, achiote,
bijol, annato, roucou

Origin and native distribution
Tropical South America

Parts used
seeds

The dry, spiny seed pod, vivid red seed arils and the seed paste of bixa or
achiote, which brightens up many kinds of food and other products.

Lipstick tree - *Bixa orellana*

We can't all possess natural beauty, my love:
The pearlescent grey-purple sheen of the dove;
The pink flushing cheeks, the plump rose-red lips,
Vampish bloodstains of Marilyn Monroe's fingertips;
The rich golden-yellow of screen goddess hair,
And of butter and cheese; don't try to compare
Those rich flavours and textures to bland margarine,
Which shows pictures of fields but is made by machine.

Grind my seeds into powder for annatto red.
For yellow bixin use my seed coat instead.
I'll outshine synthetics - I'm glad they've been banned -
You know where you are with me, fresh from the land.
My seeds can be simmered in water or fats
Then strained for a dye that could make sewer rats
Look like something belonging on *Vogue*'s hallowed pages.
My style is a classic to last through the ages.

But beauty's not only a promise, a tease;
It's fierce and it's armouring, consider these:
Brave Redskins, the Native Americans painting
Their bodies with me; conquistadors fainting
And fearful when seeing them coloured so bold.
Red's always in fashion, I'll never get old.
I'm known as achiote in Mexico;
I travel by new names wherever I go.
Annato, roucou, bixa, or lipstick tree:
My stage names will change but you'll recognise me
As the star in your midst by the strength of my glow:
Yellow, orange, or red like a kiss from Monroe.

In the Amazonian regions *Bixa orellana* is grown as a living fence and used in forestry and land rehabilitation. Worldwide it is best known as the source of yellow, orange, and red dyes for food, fabrics and cosmetics. Its star has risen since synthetic food colourings were banned in the 1950s, and the annatto or lipstick tree filled the gap in the market. It now provides around 70% of the world's natural colourings. It is proven to be non-toxic, and contains carotenoids that are high in beneficial vitamin A. You can recognise the presence of annatto by looking for E160b on ingredients labels.

A red-orange colouring known as annatto, achiote or roucou is derived from the vibrant red seeds. These are heated in liquid, often oil, to extract their red colour and subtle flavour, and the liquid is then used in cooking. Regional use varies: in Brazil the seeds are ground into powder, and in Yucatán they are mixed with other spices into a flavourful paste. For the Maya and Aztecs the plant had spiritual status as a symbol of blood, and was used to create ink for their sacred texts.

The orange-yellow dye of bixa comes from carotenoids in the spiny seed coat, and gives an inviting buttery glow to cheese, margarine and real butter, among other food products. It was once widely used for dyeing textiles, as was annatto, but they have mostly been replaced by colour-fast synthetic dyes.

The mild flavour of the dyes is a benefit, as they can be used to colour chocolate, oils, smoked fish, meats, vegetable dishes and stews without changing the taste of the main ingredients. The same applies to cosmetics, to which annatto oil adds colour and increases the antioxidant content without affecting their perfume. The carotenoid also functions as an insect repellant and prevents sunburn by filtering UV light, which is why the indigenous peoples of the Americas used this plant to make body paints.

The entire plant has traditional medicinal uses in its native Amazonian regions as well as in several South and Central American countries. This widespread therapeutic use implies that it is effective, with tangible results.

Cabbage

Botanical name
Brassica oleracea L.
(capitata group)

Common names
cabbage, savoy cabbage,
white and red cabbage

Origin and native distribution
Mediterranean region

Parts used
leaves

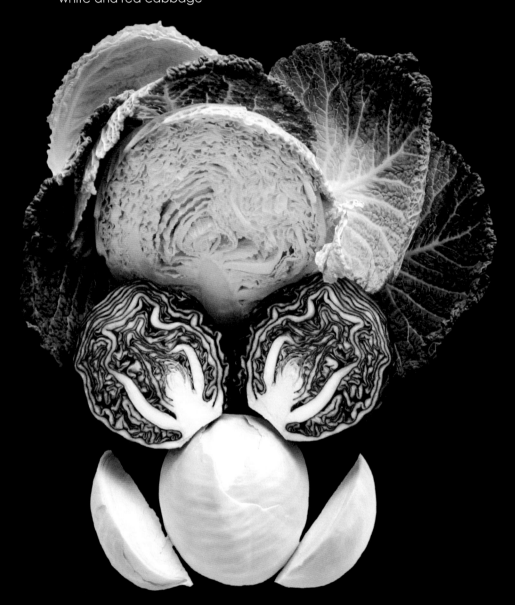

Cabbages come from the capitata group, one of the eight
cultivated varieties of *Brassica*. Top to bottom: savoy cabbage,
red cabbage and white cabbage.

Cabbage - *Brassica oleracea*

Here comes the chopper to chop off your head!
Chop - chop - chop - chop

Take crimp-haired savoy, green or white, or deep red
Chop - chop - chop - chop
Crisp guillotine sounds when your knife meets my head
Chop - chop - chop - chop
Slice quicker for coleslaw, its shards bright and thin,
For sauerkraut give me salt to ferment in.

Steam my leaves and they'll turn into versatile wraps
To envelop a scramble, a rice dish, your scraps
Jazzed up with some hot sauce - leftovers with zing!
Experiment, then you'll put less in the bin.

Cook me quick, never doom me to drowning and squeezing.
My flavour and vitamin C will be pleasing
When they're not diluted or boiled into paste;
Mistreating your brassicas so is a waste.

The sulphur within me might come out as farts;
Hold your nose by all means but don't close up your heart.
I'm caring - raw leaves can soothe hot inflamed skin.
Here's more of the clan that are worth buying in:

There's broccoli, cut up it looks like small trees,
And cauliflower, rubbed with spice or baked with cheese.
Kale and collards make strong blood with leaves rich in iron.
Kohlrabi, which look just like turnips; do try them.
Brussels sprouts are green globes clinging tight to their stalk
Like jingling bells for a fine Christmas walk;
A miniature cabbage on top - what a prize!
Romanesco's a spiralling feast for your eyes.

Despite all these cultivars, centuries old,
If our pollen mixes our ancestry bold
Will assert its true face and raise up its head;
Simply cabbage: green, white, crimped savoy, or deep red.

The mustard family or *Brassicaceae* has produced an array of vegetables which exceeds that of any other plant group. The most consumed vegetables in this family come from a single species, *Brassica oleracea*, which has been cultivated for at least 2,000 years. Originally a coastal species found growing wild on cliffs by the sea, its modern cultivars are eaten in large quantities worldwide.

They are known as the cole crops, a name derived from the Latin *caulis*, meaning *stem*. There are considered to be eight main cultivar groups which, though closely related, differ remarkably in appearance depending on where they store their starch. Cultivars include cabbages, collard greens, kale, Brussels sprouts, cauliflower, broccoli and kohlrabi. Each is a result of different modification of the leaves, stems or roots and has its own distinct history of domestication.

The brassicas are wild at heart. Despite hundreds of years of cultivation, if the pollen of different crops is allowed to mix they will revert within just a couple of generations to the wild cabbages of their ancestry. Preserving different historical varieties requires care so as not to lose the horticultural work of centuries, or miss out on the nutritional benefits and culinary pleasures of the food plants in the *Brassica oleracea* spectrum whose green, white and red vegetables nourish us with leaves, florets, stalk, buds, heads and tubers.

The distinctive bitterness or pungency of the *Brassicaceae* family is due to a class of compounds known as glucosinolates; these are antibacterial, antiviral and anti-cancerous. The vegetables are also rich in antioxidants and other essential nutrients. They provide dietary fibre which benefits the gut microbiome, and deep green varieties are rich in iron. So this single species offers a broad spectrum of health benefits to those who eat a variety of its different forms - not just broccoli and kale!

This whole family is rich in sulphur and sulphates which are missing from processed food. Intensive food processing techniques often succeed at the expense of the nutritional value of the end product. Cabbages are cheap, highly nutritious and can be grown throughout the year, so they are eaten in their local forms by cultures around the world and have been a staple food for the poor for centuries.

From the capitata group, one of the eight cultivars, we are provided with cabbage, savoy cabbage and red cabbage. These cultivars developed in Germany and were established by the 12th century. The common name cabbage derives from the French *caboche*, meaning *head*, describing the large round terminal bud that is eaten. Cabbage leaves can be cooked in ways that lift them above their earthy, unglamorous association with poverty.

Savoy cabbage has dark green puckered leaves and is often finely shredded for coleslaw. The common cabbage can be red, green or white, and has a tight head and smooth leaves. White or green cabbage is shredded and fermented to make sauerkraut, popular in Germany and Eastern European countries. While sauerkraut can be a probiotic tonic for the gut microbiome, many sauerkrauts sold in supermarkets are pasteurised to extend their shelf life. This neutralises their probiotic benefits, so look for refrigerated or unpasteurised sauerkraut.

Red cabbage is given its colour by the pigment anthocyanin. It is often used for pickling, and is also braised with spices, apple and onion as a winter dish. When cooking cabbages, speed is of the essence to preserve their vitamin C and their flavour. Letting any member of the cabbage family boil in water for too long dilutes their nutritional and sensory benefits.

Mustards (brown, black and yellow)

Botanical name	Botanical name	Botanical name
Brassica juncea (L.) Czern.	*Brassica nigra* W.D.J.Koch	*Sinapis alba* L.
Common names	Common name	Common names
brown mustard, Indian mustard, Dijon, gai choi	black mustard	yellow mustard, white mustard
Origin and native distribution	Origin and native distribution	Origin and native distribution
Central Asia	Eurasia	Eastern Mediterranean, Middle East
Parts used	Parts used	Parts used
ripe seeds, leaves	seeds, leaves	seeds, leaves

Young mustard seedlings above the smaller brown mustard
(*Brassica juncea*, left) and slightly larger black mustard seeds
(*Brassica nigra*, right), with yellow mustard seeds (*Sinapis alba*) below
and yellow mustard powder in the centre.

Brown mustard - *Brassica juncea*

The biting breath of the Himalayas
Grew *Brassica juncea*; pungent seeds
Thrown wide and warm from Central Asia to
Dijon. Find us in condiments; curries.

The money trail is clear, the silver prize
Below black pepper's gold is mine to claim:
White mustard's too, combined as second spice
Throughout the world, our condiment is named.

Why mustard? Grape must added to our seeds
With water, vinegar, egg yolk all whisked
Into a piquant sauce that bratwurst needs,
And hot dogs too; I'll perk up any dish.

Yellow mustard - *Sinapis alba*

It's not every plant that can weather the storm
And survive to speak up for itself,
But my pale little seeds can be eaten alive
And still resurrect with no one's help.
An animal's digestive tract is no party
Of pleasure, but I come out whole.
Still able to germinate after ten years,
So take heart; despite setbacks, you'll grow.
Exploring the warm realms of mustards you'll find
There are many sensations to feel.
With *Sinapis alba* your mouth is the place
Where my heat stays, and I can reveal
Sinalbin's the reason; it stays where it's put,
Doesn't vaporise up to your nose.
The chemical balance in mustard is yours
To explore; decide how hot you'll go.

The distinctive bitterness or pungency of the *Brassicaceae* family which includes cabbages, collard greens, mustard and canola oil, comes from a class of compounds known as mustard oil glycosides or glucosinolates. These are toxic to insects, but as humans are so much larger their consumption does not carry the risk of toxicity. In fact, these same hot-tasting compounds are considered to protect against cancer in humans.

Brown mustard - *Brassica juncea*

Brown mustard is native to the Himalayan region of Central Asia, and is widely grown in the Caucasus, India and China. The plant is grown for its seeds and leaves. Several seeds grow together in fruit capsules which stay closed even when ripe; these are harvested mechanically and threshed to release the seeds. Together with yellow mustard they are the second most commercially important spice after black pepper. The leaves are eaten as spring greens or potherbs, fermented, and made into pickles. The seeds can be sprouted and eaten in salads.

The name mustard comes from combining the seeds with grape must, vinegar, water, egg yolk and other regional additions to make a hot condiment that can be smooth or textured with whole or cracked seeds, such as Dijon mustard. The highly pungent seeds are used as a seasoning and to make condiments for meats, including the sauces for German bratwurst and American hot dogs.

In South India, brown mustard seeds are used to temper curries, while in Bengali and Kashmiri cuisine the oil they yield is widely used for pickling. In Italy, fruits are preserved in a syrup enlivened with the heat of mustard oil and spices. They are used like chutneys to accompany meats and cheeses. Mostarda di Cremona uses mixed fruits such as cherries, figs, apricots, plums, apples and pears. Mostarda Vicentina uses quince and Mostarda Mantovana uses sour green apples.

Black mustard - *Brassica nigra*

Black mustard is native to the Middle East and until the 1950s it was a popular choice for mustards and seasonings. When mechanical harvesting was being developed in the 1950s its popularity waned. Unlike the indehiscent (non-splitting) brown mustard, black mustard pods burst open when ripe and spill their seeds on the ground. They must be more expensively picked by hand, and could not compete with the cheaper brown mustard harvest.

Yellow mustard *- Sinapis alba*

The main difference between yellow mustard and its relatives the brown and
black mustards is the level of the glucosinolates chemical sinalbin. Glucosinolates
are shared by many brassicas, giving them their distinctive pungency. The plant
produces glucosinolates to defend itself, deterring pests which get a mouthful
of uncomfortable heat when they take a bite; the chemicals also help the plant
fight disease. Sinalbin has a persistence and stability lacking in the more volatile
sinigrin of brown and black mustards, so its heat remains in the mouth rather
than dispersing as vapour. Yellow mustard has a mild flavour but gives a lingering
heat which is released when the crushed or ground seeds are mixed with water or
wine. For humans this is pleasurable, and in small doses is also medicinal.

The seeds themselves are hardy travellers; they can pass through an animal's
digestive tract and still remain viable for ten years or more. Yellow mustard is
popular in the UK and some parts of Europe, the USA, and Canada which is
the world's leading exporter of mustard seeds. The young seedlings, just 4 to 6
centimetres high, are used alongside cress for sandwiches and salads in England,
and the mature greens are used as a potherb. Some food flavourings also include
mustard seeds.

Yellow mustard is also cultivated as an environmentally friendly manure to
enrich the soil and improve its structure and fertility, encourage microorganism
communities, and help the soil store water. The seeds are also used medicinally as
an anti-inflammatory treatment for humans.

Cannabaceae family

Hops

Botanical name
Humulus lupulus L.

Common name
hops

Origin and native distribution
Northern temperate regions

Parts used
dried cone-like female
flower clusters

The cone-shaped flower clusters used in brewing are
harvested from female hops plants.

Hops - *Humulus lupulus*

My closest relation is *Cannabis sativa*;
Both of us alter your mood.
Relaxing and calming, that's our intention,
But we're not just drugs, we are food.

My shoots can be eaten like tender asparagus,
In Sweden my fibres make cloth.
But it's been in brewing that I've made my name;
A glass of brown beer topped with froth.

My female plants only are used for beer brewing,
They wind up tall poles as they're grown.
Under the leaves hang my clusters of flowers,
Pale green pendants, shaped like a cone.

A word to the wise: too much beer is not saintly;
It sends body chemistry wild,
So that men grow top-heavy with breasts, thanks to bottles
Of beer, made from hops calm and mild.

Beer is widely sold as a talisman of masculinity but its second most important ingredient, hops, is all woman. The essential oils which give beer its aroma, the enzymes which keep it clear, and the resins which provide its bitter taste and preserve it from bacterial decay all come from the cone-shaped flower clusters on female plants. The dedicated drinker may begin to notice their own body flowering: the estrogenic effects of hops can lead to "feminization of the male body" (Rätsch), an increase in fatty tissue leading to "beer breasts".

Hops (*Humulus lupulus*) are closely related to cannabis (*Cannabis sativa*) and these two members of the *Cannabaceae* family have made their sedative influence felt around the world, their mind-altering qualities politicised and legislated both for and against.

Hops grow wild in temperate climates: across North America, Europe, into Siberia and Japan. The plant is a tall twisting climber that can reach up to 8 metres in the wild and up to 12 metres in cultivation. The first recorded cultivation of hops was in Bavaria in Southeast Germany around the 8th century, but wild hops were widely used long before then.

The ancient Greeks knew hops as an ingredient for salads and bread, while the Romans ate the shoots in the style of asparagus, as the Belgians do today. In Sweden, hops fibre was used to produce coarse cloth. Hops are also widely known as a herbal remedy. A hops pillow cured the insomnia of George III of England, and a potent soporific tisane can be made with hops and valerian. The Omaha Indian tribe applied hops to wounds, chewing it along with other ingredients and spitting the mixture into the affected area.

With its origins as a medicine and a palliative for the troubled mind, English monks first added hops to their beer in the 1500s in the hope of achieving saint-like levels of self-control. In English monasteries the distractions of carnal desires were dampened with botany and brewing as well as with prayer. The calming effects of hops flowers were well known, so monks added hops to their beer as an anaphrodisiac aid to their spiritual labours.

The monks hoped that their beer would dull the senses to the persistent sinfulness of the human mind. The other benefits hops gave, such as sparkling clarity, good bitter taste, and resistance to bacterial spoiling, allowed it to gradually replace other plants such as bog myrtle (*Myrica gale*) to become the brewer's choice.

Clusiaceae family

Mangosteen and Malabar tamarind

Botanical name
Garcinia mangostana L.

Common name
mangosteen

Origin and native distribution
Tropical Asia (Indonesia)

Parts used
fruits

Botanical name
Garcinia indica (Thouars) Choisy

Common name
Malabar tamarind, kokum

Origin and native distribution
Southwest India, Northeast India,
Southeast Asia

Parts used
fruits, seeds

Whole ripe mangosteen fruits taking a look at their
dried relative Malabar tamarind or kokum.

Mangosteen - *Garcinia mangostana*

Approach with respect this great mangosteen,
Of all the world's fruits I'm considered the queen.
Garcinia mangostana is a name of renown;
Behold these four sepals, forming my crown.

The dark glossy leaves of my evergreen tree
And my pinky-red flowers are joyful to see,
And more wonderful still is the warm fragrant air
Of sweet perfume my flowers create, and then share.

Flower changes to fruit, so leaving behind
An orange-sized ball with a red-purple rind
That houses great treasure; fair segments of white
Melting flesh to enjoy with smiles of delight.

My sweet and sour sugary taste all agree
Is delicious, though not high in vitamin C.
What I do have are chemical healers so fruity,
And my latex in pimple cream gives you more beauty.

Each tree takes a decade before fruit appears,
Teaching patience, and causing perhaps a few tears
As persuading a queen to do what you will
Requires tact and experience, knowledge and skill.

I first ruled Malaysia; my reign now extends
To more tropical lands, but to taste me depends
On your efforts. My fine flesh prefers to remain
In the warm, loving heart of my regal domain.

Clusiaceae family
Mangosteen

Botanical name
Garcinia mangostana L.
Common name
mangosteen
Origin and native distribution
Tropical Asia (Indonesia)
Parts used
fruits

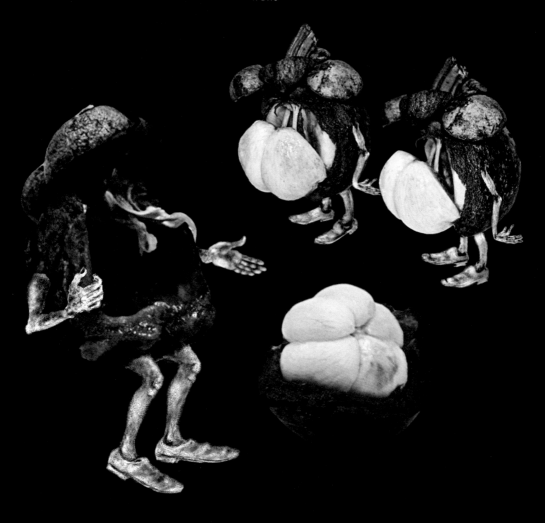

Opened fruits show their white segments of edible flesh and the beautiful
deep reddish-purple rind that holds them.

Mangosteen - *Garcinia mangostana*

The flavour of *Garcinia mangostana* is considered so good that it is often called the "queen of fruits". The flowers of this evergreen tree can be pink, green or red, and are highly scented. When they develop into fruits the sepals remain around the stalk, giving the mangosteen its characteristic four-petalled crown. The tree is very slow growing, and not easy to propagate.

The mangosteen grows to about the size of a small orange. Inside its tough reddish-purple rind are segments of juicy white flesh with a delicate sweet-sour taste. The deliciously aromatic flesh has a soft yielding texture that bruises easily and does not ship well; fresh mangosteens are rarely found far from their growing regions in tropical Asia (Indonesia). During the past two centuries the crop has been established in other tropical regions including Sri Lanka, South India, Brazil and Central America, and mangosteen orchards have been established in Queensland, Australia.

The pericarp (rind or peel) of the mangosteen is a traditional medicine for digestive disorders including dysentery and abdominal pain. It is also used to treat infected wounds and chronic ulcers. Studies of pericarp extracts have demonstrated its antioxidant, antiviral, antibacterial, antiallergic, anti-inflammatory and anti-tumour properties.

Malabar tamarind - *Garcinia indica*

Malabar tamarind is native to the tropical rainforests along the Malabar or western coast of South India and the evergreen forests of Northeastern India and Southeast Asia. The pleasingly acidic fruits are eaten raw, made into jelly and vinegar, syrup, and the drink kokum sharbat, a favourite on the west coast of India. The rinds of dried fruits are popular in fish curries, providing a unique flavour and a substitute for tamarind.

The plant is often referred to as kokum butter tree as its seeds are the source of this edible fat with a variety of uses. Kokum butter provides a substitute for ghee, butter or cocoa butter. It is useful in confectionery, especially in warm climates, as it remains hard at room temperature, and its mild odour does not intrude on the product's flavour.

Traditionally, extraction methods produce an oil or butter that is nutritionally good; the seeds are ground, steamed and pressed to release their fat. This is filtered and churned into a buttery solid, leaving a protein-rich seed cake which can be fed to livestock; a helpful by-product. However, for mass production the industry trend is towards cheaper chemical extraction. This results in a highly refined, and less nutritious, product that carries unlabelled chemicals into the food chain.

In folk medicine, kokum butter has a long history as a treatment for skin conditions and minor inflammations; it is absorbed swiftly without being greasy. It is used to moisturise dry cracked lips, skin, scalp and for the hair. Candles and soap are made from lower quality kokum butter. The tree resins are used for pigments and dyes, and one species produces the prized deep yellow gamboge.

Convolvulaceae family
Sweet potato

Botanical name
Ipomoea batatas (L.) Lam.
Common names
sweet potato, kumara

Origin and native distribution
South America
Parts used
tubers, leaves

The orange, purple and white-fleshed cultivated varieties of sweet potato tubers comparing their different colours and flavours.

Sweet potato - *Ipomoea batatas*

South America first, then Pacific Islands:
Palm-fringed Polynesia and Maori New Zealand.
Since these early adventures I've sailed like Huck Finn
To arrive in your home town: it's time to tuck in.

As *Ipomoea batatas* I'm classed
And my sugars get stronger with slow heat, not fast.
Your sweet tooth will love to chew my ruddy skin
With its treacly bubbles, oozing from within.

My tubers grow bright-fleshed in tropical soil.
You can bake me or roast me, bring me to the boil
And then mash me. For Thanksgiving sweeten me more:
Drizzle maple or honey, gold syrups galore.

I am not a true yam botanically
But it's yam I am along brown Mississippi.
So in the Deep South where they know how to cook me
Just ask for a yam and you won't overlook me.

This ancient subtropical tuber is indigenous to Colombia, Ecuador, Guatemala and Peru in South America. The Polynesians were the first outsiders to taste it. It flourished in the rich soil and warm climate of the Pacific Islands, and became a staple crop for the Maoris in New Zealand. Its Peruvian Quechua name *kumar* became *kumara* in Polynesia. The Hawaiians used to have 230 cultivars but over the centuries this diversity has been lost, and only 24 are known there today.

From South America, the sweet potato was carried by the Portuguese and Spanish conquistadors to Europe, Africa and Asia. The name *batata* from the Taino peoples of the Caribbean was changed to *patata* by the Spanish, and this became *potato* in English. By the end of the 15th century the tuber was established in the Philippines and China. Today, China grows the majority of the world's sweet potatoes and they are one of the largest food crops worldwide.

Ranging from oblong to almost round, the colour of the skin doesn't vary as much as the vibrant flesh inside. White-fleshed varieties are less sweet than the yellow and orange, whose radiant glow is generated by carotenoid pigments. The purple varieties have a delicate nutty taste. The sweet potato cooks more swiftly than white potatoes, *Solanum tuberosum*, so it is ideal for boiling, steaming, mashing, and making into soups. They can be batter-fried as tempura, or dried for later use.

The more starchy, savoury *aja* type is favoured in the Caribbean and Africa. Across the rest of the world the sweet *batata* type is preferred. During the cooking process, an enzyme in the *batata* tuber breaks down its starch into maltose, which is a third as sweet as table sugar. When slowly baked in its skin the flesh can burst out into sugary bubbles which become caramelised, almost treacly. This makes it the perfect vegetable to eat if you have sweet cravings, as it satisfies the appetite while avoiding the refined sugars that can contribute to diabetes. It is a high-energy food and a source of protein, potassium, fibre, and vitamins A (especially in the orange varieties), B and C.

These tubers blend well with other sweet-fleshed crops such as squash and carrots, and provide a tasty contrast to acidic tomatoes, pungent chilli, lively lemongrass and lime. They complement a variety of herbs and spices. Their sweetness can be emphasised in pies and baked goods, breads, jams, ice cream and dulce de batata, a kind of caramel. The starch from sweet potatoes is made into dang myun noodles in Korea and imo miso and harusame noodles in Japan. Sweet potatoes are fermented into the alcoholic drinks awamori, shochu, masato, and chicha.

Sweet potatoes have heart-shaped or deeply lobed leaves and even these are good to eat, although most people miss this delicacy. Many other root crops have nutritious leaves that are discarded before they reach our shops, or are mistakenly cast aside in the kitchen. Not all food plant leaves are edible, but it's worth checking that you're not binning half your meal before you cook it.

In the USA, the sweet potato forms an important part of the Thanksgiving feast and of the soul food of the Deep South. Thanks to 1930s marketing campaigns it is commonly known as *yam* in the USA, which derives from a West African word meaning *to eat*, but yams are from a different botanical family (*Dioscoreaceae*).

Whatever you call them, these tubers should be kept out of the fridge. When too cold they can develop hardcore, where the centre stays hard when cooked, resisting all attempts to soften its displeasure.

Beyond their culinary uses, the tubers are used as an industrial source of starch and ethanol, and are combined with natural fibres to make biodegradable plastic for Toyota cars.

Cucurbitaceae family
Pumpkin seed

Botanical name
Cucurbita pepo L.

Common names
pumpkin, summer squash

Origin and native distribution
North America, Central America

Parts used
young fruits, seeds

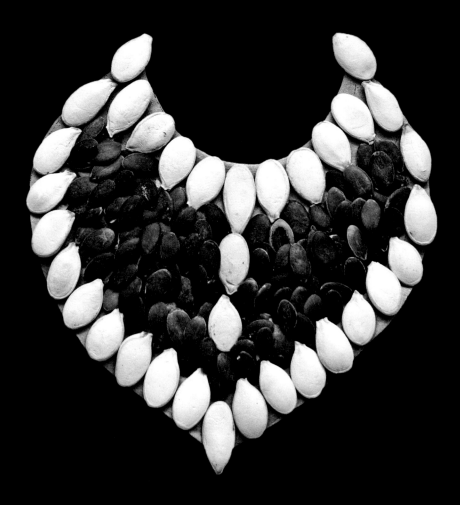

White unshelled and green shelled pumpkin seeds. A wide
variety of squashes, including the traditional Hallowe'en pumpkin,
have edible seeds which are usually eaten toasted.

Pumpkin seed - *Cucurbita pepo*

When mastodons with hairy toes
Gallumphed around in Mexico
The temperatures were icy cold.
These animals grew big and bold.
They used their elephantine ears
To stay alert to spiky spears
That humans threw when hunting meat.
But mastodons, what did they eat?

They didn't eat the human folk.
They didn't eat the gold egg yolk.
They didn't make kebabs, although
Those tusks seem perfect skewers, no!
They wanted food their trunks could grip.
They wanted food that they could slip
Into their mouths and crunch to mush,
So they ate pumpkin, summer squash.

Quite early in the Holocene
Small wild pumpkins were on the scene.
Their seeds were bitter, humans chose
The sweetest kinds and planted those.
Palaeontologists have found
Mastodon tummies in the ground,
Preserved inside the mastodon,
Unearthed for us to look upon.

It's there they found the evidence,
The pumpkin seeds that show good sense
In food had not yet gone extinct,
For pumpkin seeds are full of zinc.
They give you energy to run,
They're handy things to feast upon,
While pumpkin flesh is bright and sweet
For mastodons with hairy feet.

We are now living in a geological epoch known as the Holocene, which began around 11,500 years ago when the glaciers of the last ice age retreated and the world entered a warmer phase. Mastodons and woolly mammoths tramped their heavy steps across Mexico, not yet pushed into extinction by rising temperatures.

These large mammals had a limited ability to register bitter tastes. The wild pumpkins of this time were not sweet, and had seeds full of bitter-tasting chemicals, the plant's defence system against predation. While smaller mammals found these chemicals unpalatable and toxic when bitten into, the mastodons swallowed the seeds whole. Their size protected them against the small dose of toxins, and the seeds passed through their digestive system. The seeds were dispersed within a plug of mastodon manure as fertiliser, helping squashes to thrive as a species.

When humans began cultivating squashes they chose the least bitter seeds to plant. Over time, this led to the delicious pumpkin seeds and large, sweet-fleshed varieties we know today. When mastodons and mammoths became extinct, humans continued their work of ensuring that *Cucurbita pepo* and other varieties continued to swell and grow sweet. The seeds are an excellent source of zinc and the green coating is rich in chlorophyll. The fruit's yellow-orange flesh is a sign of carotenoids, which promote healthy growth and eyesight, and of beta-carotene which is a precursor of vitamin A.

Cucurbita pepo is one of the oldest domesticated plants and, along with other edible squashes, was one of the "three sisters"; the squash, beans, and maize which were the foundation of nutrition for America's native population before European colonisation. Hundreds of cultivars of squashes, gourds and pumpkins are available, and their size, shape, skin texture and colour vary wildly. The spectrum includes orange, red, green, yellow, white and blue-grey. The fruits are cooked as a vegetable and used in soups, stews, breads, and as a savoury or sweet pie filling. In Mexico the roasted seeds are called pepitas.

The original Hallowe'en pumpkin was a turnip, and the tradition came from an Irish myth. A man known as Stingy Jack found a way to achieve riches by cheating the Devil, but when he died the Devil had his revenge. Jack found himself not only excluded from Heaven, but barred from Hell also, and his ghost was doomed to restless wandering on earth for all time. To scare Jack away from their homes, Irish people began carving frightening faces into turnips, known as jack-o'-lanterns. The tradition was carried across the Atlantic with Irish immigrants to the United States, who transferred their carving skills to the native pumpkins.

Hallowe'en is rooted in the ancient Celtic festival of Samhain: the end of the year, when the veil between worlds is most thin and the souls of the dead can more easily cross over. As Christianity established itself in Europe, it dominated long-standing pagan festivals and sacred sites in order to transfer devotions to the new religion. In the 8th century, the Roman Catholic Church moved All Saints Day to 1 November (the Celtic New Year) so that All Hallows' Eve fell on Samhain. The lanterns to ward off Stingy Jack were incorporated into the ongoing Samhain traditions to ward off spirits wandering abroad. Over the years the celebration of Hallowe'en grew more enthusiastic in America, and eventually crossed the Atlantic again to become a trend in Britain.

Cucurbitaceae family
Karela and kaksa

Botanical name
Momordica charantia L.

Botanical name
Momordica dioica Roxb. ex Willd.

Common names
karela, bitter gourd, bitter melon

Common names
kaksa, teasel gourd

Origin and native distribution
India, Tropical Asia

Origin and native distribution
Tropical Asia

Parts used
fruits

Parts used
fruits, leaves, tender shoots

The soft, spiny *Momordica dioica* teasel gourd sitting on the
cultivated varieties of *Momordica charantia*: the ridged and toothy
Indian variety and the warty, undulating Chinese variety.

Karela and kaksa
- Momordica charantia and *Momordica dioica*

Momordica charantia's my name.
China, India, Asia; there my fame
Comes from bitterness being understood;
A sign of vitamins that do you good.
Inside this warty, jagged, gnarly skin
Brown seeds and bright red arils wait within.
Cut me in half from top to bottom; take
My seeds and fibre out; then you can make,
Perhaps, the Chinese speciality
Which pairs fermented black soybeans and me.
Too bitter? A salt water bath will soothe
Before I'm stuffed, fried, pickled, boiled or stewed.
Young or mature, this bitterness of mine
Won't sweeten, but when cooking, that's just fine.
Like insulin I move your food's glucose
From blood to other cells; safely it flows.
Momordica dioica, bitter-sweet:
A spiny relative, just steam and eat
Or, as they do by River Ganges' banks,
Prepare a curry, offer up your thanks.

Karela - *Momordica charantia*

Karela requires some preparation, but is highly nutritious. Before it is cooked, the fruit is cut open, its seeds and fibre removed, and the remaining flesh soaked in salt, steamed or parboiled to reduce its bitterness. The sour flavours of tamarind and tomato are also used to mask the bitterness. Only unripe fruits are eaten; they are used in savoury dishes such as soups, stews, curries, stir fries and chop suey, and in pickles. The traditional Chinese way to serve them is with fermented black soybeans. Some varieties produce miniature fruits which are popular as stuffed vegetables in South Asia. The plant's leaves and young shoots can also be cooked as a vegetable or potherb.

The undulating, warty Chinese cultivated variety and the jagged, toothy Indian variety are examples of the plant's many different guises. The fruits vary in size from 6 to 30 centimetres depending on the variety, and in colour from white to different shades of green. This popular plant is used as a vegetable and as part of the traditional medicines of India and China. Its phytochemicals are seen to have a wide range of health benefits, especially in moderating blood sugar levels in diabetes and related problems.

Kaksa - *Momordica dioica*

Kaksa or teasel gourd produces soft spiny green fruits that are eaten young, along with their roots, leaves, and shoots. The flesh is bitter-sweet and requires no pre-cooking treatment; it can be steamed like other vegetables. Despite having many medicinal benefits it is not widely cultivated; it is grown on the fertile Indo-Gangetic regions of India, Pakistan, Nepal and Bangladesh.

Cucurbitaceae family
Chayote

Botanical name
Sicyos edulis Jacq.

Common names
chayote, vegetable pear, chocho

Origin and native distribution
Central America

Parts used
fruit, tubers, young shoots

Chayotes getting ready for the pot, left to right: the pale green
gently spiny variety and the darker green smooth-skinned variety, both
with slightly ribbed skin and the characteristic swelling base

Cucurbitaceae family

Chayote - *Sicyos edulis*

Sicyos edulis, chayote or chocho,
Or vegetable pear; wherever you go
The sound of my name on each person's lips
Is music that slides, shifts, echoes and slips.
My swelling behind like scallops of flesh
Conceals just one seed that is large, soft and fresh.
My juicy nutrients flow to this heart
So full of flavour, the tastiest part.
Like many plants it's not only my fruits
That sustain you; try tubers, leaves and shoots.
To grow more chayote keep me whole and sound,
Then nestle my fruit, intact, underground.
This rare method suits my unique species;
A one-seeded squash, a mildness to please
All who cook with me. Aztecs began it,
Now I'm re-named all over the planet.

Sicyos edulis, commonly called chayote, vegetable pear, or chocho, is unique among fruits. The single almond-shaped seed inside it cannot be dried and saved like most seeds, and it cannot be planted separately. The seed is soft, and draws into itself the fruit's nutrients and water, making it a tender and tasty delicacy. This unusual behaviour means that to propagate chayote, the whole fruit must be planted, as it germinates within itself.

Like other squash, the chayote grows on strong, clinging tendrils that arise from tuberous roots, which spread rapidly across the ground or climb like vines. Chayote was first cultivated by the Aztecs and Maya in Central America. When Europeans arrived in the 15th century they spread the fruit to South America, the Caribbean and Europe. Later it was taken to Asia, Africa, and Australia, and it now grows in subtropical regions around the world. Its common name declares its origin, as the Spanish word *chayote* is derived from the Nahuatl name for the plant, *chaoytl*.

All parts of the chayote can be eaten, including the flowers and leaves. The tuberous roots can be cooked as a vegetable or candied, and the young shoots and tendrils are eaten in a similar way to asparagus. The fruit has a mild, slightly sweet flavour, and the mature, swelling seeds are the tastiest part. They are used like apples in pies and tarts, but also like potatoes: mashed, baked, deep fried, and used in stews and curries. They can be stuffed, pickled, and made into sweetmeats. Their mellow flavour allows them to blend with other ingredients, and they can simply be eaten raw.

In addition to being nutritious, chayote contains many bioactive compounds which are being researched for their potential to provide pharmaceuticals to treat a range of medical conditions.

Japanese persimmon and Chocolate pudding fruit

Botanical name
Diospyros kaki L.f.

Common names
Japanese persimmon,
persimmon, kaki

Origin and native distribution
East Asia, cultivated in China
and Japan

Parts used
ripe fruits

Botanical name
Diospyros nigra (J.F.Gmel.) Perr.

Common names
chocolate pudding fruit,
black sapote, black persimmon

Origin and native distribution
Central America

Parts used
ripe fruits

At the feet of the firm, swollen ripe fruit of kaki or
Japanese persimmon (*Diospyros kaki*) sit whole and opened
chocolate pudding fruits (*Diospyros nigra*).

Japanese persimmon - *Diospyros kaki*

Evergreen in humid heat,
From flower to fruit my trees
Belong to precious darkness,
Relatives of ebony.

Your face might squint and pucker
If impatience makes you eat
My unripe fruits - have patience,
Wait until I'm ripe and sweet.

I swell into a lantern
With a glowing orange light
That guides your hunger onwards;
Pick me up and take a bite.

Chocolate pudding fruit - *Diospyros nigra*

Do you like chocolate?
Well of course you do.
It's rich and delicious,
And versatile too.
Inside my green skin
Is a brown pulpy goo
Just like chocolate pudding -
It tastes okay too.
Just add a good squeeze
Of citrus to me
And behold, I'm dessert!
You can even drink me.
But please don't expect
A true cocoa hit.
Diospyros nigra
Can't quite manage it.

Japanese persimmon - *Diospyros kaki*

Diospyros kaki, persimmon or kaki, is native to East Asia and is widely cultivated in Japan and China. The Israeli variety, called Sharon fruit, has been bred for sweetness, without the bitter, acidic tannins that characterise other varieties. The glowing orange flesh of persimmons is a sign of the fruit's high vitamin A content.

The ripe fruits are peeled for use in fruit salads, desserts, jams and ice creams. The dried fruits, called hoshigaki, are delicacies in Japan, and they are used in a sweet spiced Korean punch called sujonggwa. The crystallised fruits or powdered dried peels are used as an alternative to sugar.

The high tannin content makes biting into an unripe persimmon a lip-pursing, tongue-contracting experience. The fruits are picked and sold unripe as the soft ripe fruits do not keep well. The astringent tannins have their uses; the young tree bark can be used as a fishing aid, poisoning the water and making dead fish float to the surface; the tannins also dye the nets used to collect the fish.

Chocolate pudding fruit - *Diospyros nigra*

Diospyros nigra is an evergreen tree native to Central America. The trees have been naturalised in Asia and are cultivated in countries that can provide the heat and humidity in which they thrive. Commonly known as black sapote, chocolate pudding fruit and black persimmon, the fruit has mottled green skin that turns brown when fully ripe. The fruit pulp within the green skin is mushy, and varies from deep chocolate brown to black. It can appear dirty rather than appetising. Its bland sweet flavour is usually perked up by lime, lemon or orange juice. It is at its best when combined with other ingredients in desserts, ice cream, preserves, smoothies and other dishes, and can be fermented into a liqueur. Unripe fruits are cooked as a vegetable.

Both *Diospyros nigra* and *Diospyros kaki* are related to the ebony trees prized for their dark wood.

Fabaceae family

Peanut

Botanical name
Arachis hypogaea L.

Common names
peanut, groundnut, earthnut

Origin and native distribution
South and Central America

Parts used
seeds

Shelled and unshelled peanuts: smaller varieties mainly
produce oil and the larger cocktail variety are popular for eating.
Below, peanuts help each other out of their papery shells.

Fabaceae family

Peanut - *Arachis hypogaea*

I'm not to blame, it's human greed that forms
The skeletons that lurk within my shell.
I'm open hearted, nourishing and good,
But mastery of destiny is rare.
In hell on earth, in slave ships I first sailed.
From South America, those Portuguese
Who dealt in flesh took me to Africa.
I fed the grieving people left behind
With groundnut stew, for energy to hope.
I kept hearts beating in the crowded dark
As ships took stolen people to my lands,
And me along with them, borne on the swell.

Before the sixteenth century disturbed
The purity of the Atlantic's waves
With horrors that make tears fall to this day,
There was no tarnish on this good plant's name.
For centuries I'd fed my people well.
I do so still, but modern man's desire
For profit - safety ranked below shelf life -
Has made me scapegoat, so I warn you now:
If I'm stored carelessly, or past my prime
Then mould, with aflatoxins, grows on me.
Despite my proteins and my healthy oils
I'm not immortal; nor are you my friend.

The peanut has bounced back and forth across the Atlantic for 500 years, but has been grown for at least 3,500 years in its native South and Central America, where it was an important part of the diet of the indigenous peoples.

With the continent of America being almost peanut-shaped itself, the swelling landmasses of North and South separated by a narrow isthmus like two seeds in their shell, it would have been easy for peanuts to cross this narrow land border. However instead of taking the easiest route by land to North America, peanuts went on a long and adventurous journey and were perhaps the first example of excessive food miles.

After the Portuguese reached Brazil in 1500, their slave traders took peanuts across the Atlantic to Africa where they became a major part of the West and Central African diet (groundnut stew). The Portuguese also took them to India (Bombay mix), while the Spanish took them to Asia (satay). It was from Africa via the Atlantic that they entered North America. India and China are the largest producers today.

As they were challenging to grow and harvest, until the 19th century North America only used peanuts to feed animals and the Southern poor. After the Civil War, advances in technology made peanuts economically viable and by the 20th century demand was high. A hero of peanut promotion was the botanist George Washington Carver, who recognised its benefits as a rotation crop in the Southeast where cotton was suffering from boll weevil infestations and soil depletion. He recognised that peanuts had nitrogen-fixing properties that reduced the need for fertilisers by putting nitrogen back into the soil. Carver generated over 300 culinary and industrial uses for the crunchy little seeds, but he didn't invent peanut butter.

Peanut butter was an ancient food of the Incas. The modern versions were developed in the 1880s and 1890s in Canada and America by at least three people independently, including John Harvey Kellogg the cereal pusher. It was recommended as a rich source of protein, especially for elderly people whose teeth weren't up to chewing meat, and became an important and portable source of protein during the two World Wars which established it in Europe.

America gave the world the classic combination of PB&J: peanut butter and jelly (US) or jam (UK). However, many peanut butters are highly salted and unnecessarily sugared, and emulsified, usually with palm oil, for a spreadable consistency even after sitting in the jar for weeks. Unadulterated versions can be found which are 100% peanut and a healthier choice; they will require stirring as the peanut oil naturally rises to the top.

Peanuts are not having a good decade. Once top of the guest list for snacks at parties and bars, these days peanuts are experiencing social death, and the label "contains nuts" has changed from a selling point to a warning. The industry expectation that food in packets should have a long shelf life is often the cause of the problem. Peanuts go mouldy with age and produce carcinogenic aflatoxins, which can affect eaters quite separately to the risk of anaphylaxis from allergic reaction. Aflatoxins can cause urticaria; rashes, swelling, asthma and eczema. This is another reason to buy the best peanuts and peanut butter you can afford, to support careful production methods and reduce the risk that mouldy peanuts will have slipped in.

Despite being at the centre of so much nut-negative publicity, the peanut is not a nut but a legume. It is related to beans and peas, hence the "pea" in its common name. Even its yellow flowers with reddish veins are shaped like a typical pea flower. After pollination the fruit grows into a young pod which bends earthwards, while the stalks lengthen into long tendrils which push the pods into the ground where they mature until they are three to seven centimetres long, with up to six seeds or peanuts inside. The *hypogaea* in the Latin name *Arachis hypogaea* means *under the earth*, and peanut's common names of groundnut and earthnut also distinguish it from other legumes which grow above ground. Like all legumes they form a symbiotic relationship with nitrogen-fixing soil bacteria. These bacteria form nodules on the plant root which enriches the soil through nitrogen fixation.

When kept in their pods and protected from heat and damp, peanuts can be stored for up to ten months. Peanuts are full of nutrients; rich in proteins, vitamins (including B vitamins), minerals such as copper and chromium, and high in unsaturated oleic and linoleic acids. They are famed for their oil content and cold-pressed peanut oil is the most popular choice for stir fry cooking. As long as you're not allergic, it's time to give peanuts another chance.

Fabaceae family
Chickpea

Botanical name
Cicer arietinum L.
Common names
chickpea, garbanzo, Bengal gram
Origin and native distribution
Middle East, Mediterranean region
Parts used
ripe dry seeds

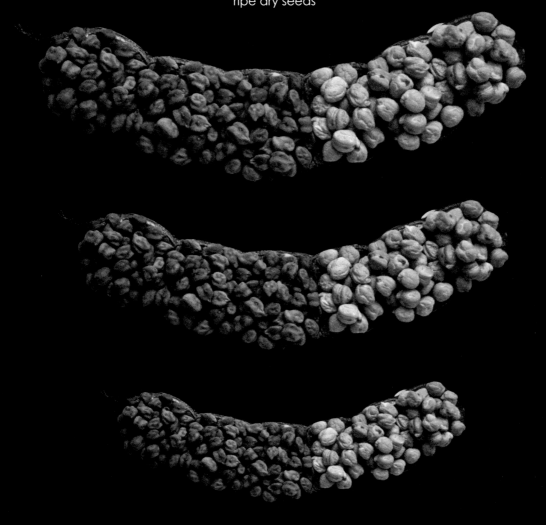

The two cultivated varieties of chickpea, left to right: the small
dark-coloured Desi, grown in Asia, Iran, Ethiopia and Mexico,
and the large cream-coloured Kabuli, grown in the Middle East
and Mediterranean region.

Chickpea - *Cicer arietinum*

Let's start with the name, *Cicer arietinum*,
That's used to describe my remarkable look.
You won't find another legume quite like me,
I'm unique in every botanical book.

Arietinum means *ram-like*; just think of Aries
The ram constellation in the sky at night.
With a fiery urge to take action, but
Needing energy; fuel to keep flames burning bright.

My knobbly shape brings curled rams horns to mind.
Look closely: can you see the head of a ram?
If my name is a mouthful then you can just say
Chickpea or garbanzo, in India I'm gram.

Centuries' worth of good recipes beckon.
I'm versatile, bursting with protein and oil.
A flavourful seed to stoke dormant embers,
To keep your flames bright and your hopes on the boil.

The chickpea originates in the Southeast of Turkey and Northern Syria. It was one of the first legumes to be domesticated, with cultivation going back at least 6,000 years. Around 2,000 years ago it was introduced into India, and in the 16th century it was taken to Latin America by the Spanish and Portuguese.

The probable wild ancestor of this cultivated plant is *Cicer reticulatum*, and today two main varieties are grown. The Desi variety is the most similar to the wild chickpea and is mainly grown in Iran, Asia, Ethiopia and Mexico. This variety has bushy plants with violet flowers, and produces small, dark chickpeas with an angular shape and a tough seed coat. The plants of the Kabuli variety are more upright with white flowers, and the chickpeas are larger and cream-coloured with a thin seed coat. They are the most common type in the Mediterranean and Middle East.

The botanical name, *Cicer arietinum*, refers to the seed's resemblance to the head or skull of a ram; the word for *ram*, *aries*, also gives its name to a constellation. *Cicer* became *ceci* in Italy, *pois chiches* in French, and *chickpeas* in English. In India, the chickpea is known as Bengal gram when whole, chana dhal when split, and besan when ground into flour.

The chickpea has become a staple food, and is the most important legume in India. It is highly nutritious, with about 17% protein and around 5% fat, a nutty taste and rough texture that makes it a versatile and sustaining food. Chickpeas are often sold dried to be soaked before cooking, or pre-cooked and sold ready to use in cans or jars. When the seeds are sprouted for 30 to 48 hours their vitamin C content doubles to the extent that these germinated chickpeas can cure scurvy.

Chickpeas are eaten in soups, salads, stews and curries, and the flour is used in pancakes, dumplings, noodles, sweetmeats and other dishes. Hummus and falafel are classic chickpea dishes from the Middle East. The roasted seeds and roasted roots can be ground and used as a coffee substitute. The seeds can also be eaten fresh, when they are green with a lemony taste. Aquafaba, the liquid from cooked or canned chickpeas and other pulses, can be used as a replacement for eggs as a binding ingredient in cakes and desserts.

Lentil

Botanical name
Lens culinaris Medik.

Common name
lentil

Origin and native distribution
Middle East, Central Asia

Parts used
seeds

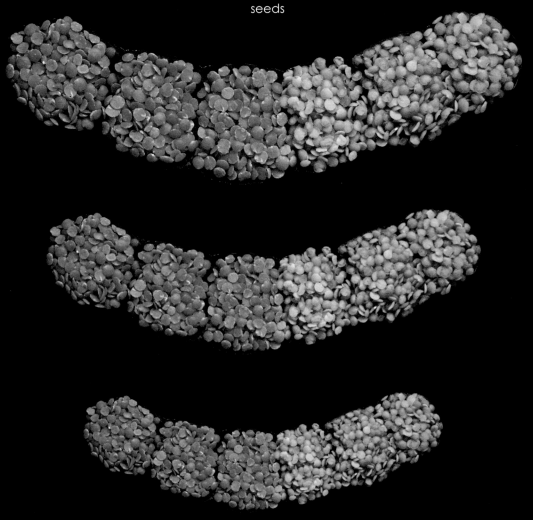

Red and yellow lentils are the brightest in the wide spectrum
of lentil colours, which includes green, brown and black.

Lentil - *Lens culinaris*

From the Middle East's garden, the great Fertile Crescent,
Come *Lens culinaris*, a valuable present.
We've often been planted with barley and wheat,
And if you've never tried us you're in for a treat.

These colourful lentils jump into your pot;
Add chilli and spice if you like your food hot.
Our flat little discs or our spherical seeds
Will satisfy all of your energy needs.
B vitamins help if you're feeling anaemic
And anyone who has been hypoglycaemic
Should know that our energy really lasts long;
Being one quarter protein we'll help you stay strong.
Legumes are high-fibre, which helps you let go
Of poo leaving your body, all part of life's flow.

To a watery soup we add body and weight.
Our presence makes curries and salads taste great.
Bake bread with our flour for a loaf you will savour
Or simmer us slow for a dal full of flavour.
From velvety mush to cooked through but still whole,
You'll learn which lentil's right for each recipe's role.
Red, yellow, bright orange and round glossy black;
Green and brown have selenium, a mineral folks lack
But can find in some foods; so don't limit yourself
To one colour, store rainbows on your kitchen shelf.

Lentils are one of the earliest crops, cultivated since between 7000 to 5000 BCE. Traditionally grown with wheat and barley, they remain little changed by modern agriculture. In addition to being popular with humans their foliage provides forage for animals. Like other legumes their seeds grow in pods which are short, flat and broad, rarely longer than two centimetres, and usually containing two seeds.

The common name lentil comes from the word *lens*, which from the 17th century was used to mean a doubly convex piece of glass which echoes the lentil's shape. Lentils offer a spectrum of colours and sizes. They cook more quickly than most beans and peas thanks to their flatter shape, as the water only needs to penetrate a millimetre or two to soften the legume. The seeds can be green, orange, black, brown, yellow or red.

Lentils are packed with nutrients. They contain 25% protein which makes them a good source of energy and they are also rich in B vitamins, iron, fibre, potassium and complex carbohydrates. They contain almost no fat. These qualities make lentils an excellent source of nourishment for vegetarians and a recommended dietary supplement for infants, invalids and nursing mothers.

During the month of Lent in the Middle East, Christian families cook Mujaddara and Mudardara; two variations of a dish combining lentils, rice and caramelised onions. Mujaddara has a softer puréed consistency while Mudardara has more whole grains, achieved by varying the proportions of lentils and rice. In Lebanon they are eaten year-round by all faiths, and are traditionally served with a cabbage salad (salatit malfouf).

Lentils are a handy staple for busy cooks as, unlike other legumes, they do not need to be soaked overnight. They cook comparatively quickly, from 20 to 45 minutes depending on the lentil and the dish. All legumes can be cooked in advance and reheated. Lentils are an incredible vehicle for flavour, carrying spices, cream or coconut cream and vegetables while imparting their own distinct tastes. *Dal* or *dhal* translates simply as *lentils*, and recipes from different regions call for specific spice combinations, types of lentils and cooking times. A simple dal can be made using quick-cooking red lentils, and they add thickness, flavour and nutrients to soups and stews.

Whichever you use, when cooking lentils it is important to wash them thoroughly first; they are often dried in the sun, exposing them to contact with birds, beasts and insects. Salt is usually added at the end of the cooking time rather than the start, to prevent the legumes from becoming tough.

Fabaceae family
Pea

Botanical name
Pisum sativum L.

Common names
pea, garden pea, field pea

Origin and native distribution
Middle East, Mediterranean region

Parts used
green fruits, dry seeds

Whole garden pea pods admiring the treasure that lies within;
freshly shelled seeds known as peas.

Fabaceae family

Pea - *Pisum sativum*

Before electric freezers
Stopped fresh foods decomposing,
What mattered was the dried foods;
And that's why we were chosen.

Although our growing season,
Like ourselves, is short and sweet,
Once dried then rehydrated
We'll spring lively to our feet.

It's been ten thousand years since
Our green tendrils curled and spread,
From the fertile Middle East
We made our way along the Med.

Fresh or dried or in the pod,
However we appear,
A wealth of vitamins are
Packed inside one small green sphere.

So when you see us offered,
Please do give peas a chance.
We'll hurry platewards, rolling
In a happy dinner dance.

Fresh green peas, edible-pod peas and dried peas are all *Pisum sativum*, processed for eating now or later. Garden or green peas are immature seeds still in the process of collecting nutrients and sugars from the plant, making them sweet and tender. They are eaten fresh or cooked from frozen. A serving of cooked green peas provides a hefty portion of our daily requirement of vitamins B and C, along with other nutrients and fibre.

When mature, the seeds become dry and less sweet, but higher in protein and starch. These field peas are often known as split peas. The dried seed coat can be blue-green, yellow, pale brown or white. They can be cooked in soups and stews, fermented, or ground into powder to make a versatile flour. Dried peas have been called "poor man's meat" as they offer an affordable source of essential nutrients; not only protein, but vitamins and minerals such as iron and zinc. Despite being an ideal solution to common nutritional deficiencies worldwide, they are currently underutilised and underpromoted, especially compared to cereals.

There is archaeological evidence that peas have been used by humans for around 10,000 years. The pea's wild ancestor was a climbing vine, which humans cultivated into bushes for easy harvesting. Peas were domesticated in the Middle East, had spread throughout Europe by around 5,000 years ago, and reached China just under 2,000 years ago. Peas became important because they could be easily dried and stored, providing a secure source of nutrition if fresh food was scarce. The growing season of peas is short, so drying the late spring harvest fed people all year round before the invention of canning and freezing. Some canned peas contain simply peas and water, while processed marrowfat and mushy peas can include a cocktail of preservatives, sugar, salt, and colourings.

The most recent innovation is the cultivation of edible-pod peas, grown as early as the 17th century for a sweeter and less fibrous pod which can be eaten whole. The varieties we know as mange tout, snow peas or sugar snap peas are a recent addition to our plates, widely cultivated since 1979. The curling tendrils of pea shoots and their leaves can be eaten, as can the flowers and sprouted seeds.

Peas played an important role in the science of genetics. The father of genetics, Gregor Mendel, a friar at the Augustinian Abbey of St. Thomas in Brünn (Brno), crossed pea plants in the 1860s. Through these experiments he gained an understanding of how specific genetic traits are inherited. This shone a light on evolution, plant breeding and biodiversity. The discoveries made thanks to pea plants remain important in our understanding of the natural world, and the effects of human intervention through agriculture. Similar experiments with pea plants were conducted by Charles Darwin.

Winged bean

Botanical name
Psophocarpus tetragonolobus (L.) DC.

Common names
winged bean, Goa bean

Origin and native distribution
possibly Southeastern Asia
and East Tropical Africa

Parts used
green pods, ripe seeds, flowers
young leaves, tuberous roots

The extravagantly fringed winged bean fruits.

Winged bean - *Psophocarpus tetragonolobus*

Behold the fringes on my dress!
My fashion sense is effortless.
I love these feathered wings of mine,
On catwalks they would look divine.

But I'm not just a pretty face,
I've star potential for your race;
You humans who eat many things
Could feast, in future, on my wings.

"One Species Supermarket" - yes!
Diversity that you will bless
When roots, pods, seeds and green parts too
Dress up your meal times, feeding you.

For protein, my pods, seeds, and roots
Will satisfy you, and my shoots
Are green and tasty, cooked or raw.
Seeds, oil, leaves - nutrients galore!

The winged bean is an equatorial legume, cultivated extensively in the countries situated between India and Papua New Guinea, and in some African countries. It is currently cultivated on a small scale, but it has potential to become a major food source. It is just one of many underutilised plants which could redress the widespread nutritional poverty that is the result of too many people eating too few species.

Psophocarpus tetragonolobus is referred to as "One Species Supermarket" as it provides a spectrum of nutrients, and all parts of the plant can be eaten. Like other legumes it fixes nitrogen in the soil, enriching the land in which it grows, making it a good choice for both small and large scale farming.

The different parts of the winged bean provide a pleasing array of flavours. The tender pods, seeds and tubers are all very high in protein and micronutrients. The immature pods can be eaten raw or cooked, and have a mild flavour similar to asparagus. They are also a good source of calcium, vitamin A and iron. The tuberous roots can also be eaten raw or cooked, and have a slightly nutty sweet taste. The mature seeds can be dried and roasted, pressed for oil, or fermented into tempeh. The leaves and flowers can also be eaten as a vegetable. What are we waiting for?

Fabaceae family
Fenugreek

Botanical name
Trigonella foenum-graecum L.

Origin and native distribution
Mediterranean region, Middle East

Common names
fenugreek, methi

Parts used
seeds, leaves

Fresh leaves and seeds of fenugreek, a versatile and mysterious spice.

Fenugreek - *Trigonella foenum-graecum*

Trigonella foenum-graecum.
Quite long words, eh? Can you speak 'em?
You could just call me fenugreek
Or methi, just a little squeak.

Come set my potent flavour free
In leafy salads or in tea.
Grind up my seeds with spices for
Great curry - you'll be back for more.

My medical potential's been
Healing for commoner and queen.
My potent yellow seeds were shut
Into the tomb of young King Tut.

I stay out of the graves these days,
As there are many better ways
To share my green and tasty leaves,
And small but strongly-flavoured seeds.

Fenugreek's aromatic compounds are mysterious and complex. They lend themselves to curry powders, stews and other savoury dishes, but can also be used in low concentrations to invoke some of the most expensive sweet flavours. Fenugreek essential oil or ground seeds are used in imitation vanilla and maple syrup, and in rum, liquorice and butterscotch flavourings. The name *foenum-graecum* translates as *Greek hay*, reminding us that fenugreek also serves as fodder for animals as well as for humans.

Fenugreek's white flowers have no stalks of their own, so they grow in the leaf axils and develop into slim pods containing up to twenty yellow-brown seeds. These seeds can be sprouted, or soaked and cooked. They are used sparingly like spices, as their flavour can be quite bitter. The seed's aroma changes when cooked, and it is an essential ingredient in the Bengali and Eastern Indian five-spice blend panch phoron, made from seeds of fenugreek, black mustard, cumin, nigella and fennel. Fresh fenugreek leaves are used as a potherb in India, and are used along with the seeds to make a tisane.

The Assyrians and ancient Egyptians cultivated the plant for culinary and medicinal use, and the seeds were used to make a yellow dye. The seeds were found in the tomb of Tutankhamun, dating from around 1325 BCE. Traditional remedies include taking the seeds to relieve digestive problems such as dysentery and acid reflux. Fenugreek has been especially indicated for women, to prevent menstrual cramps, regulate the hormones, induce labour and increase the flow of breast milk. Fenugreek tisane made with cold water has been used to treat diseases of the lungs.

Recently proven properties of fenugreek include its ability to regulate blood sugar and cholesterol levels, making it an aid to people at risk from diabetes or heart conditions. It is also active in defending the body against viral and microbial infection, and controlling inflammation and the growth of tumours.

Fabaceae family
Broad Bean

Botanical name
Vicia faba L.

Common names
broad bean, fava bean

Origin and native distribution
Middle East

Parts used
seeds, unripe pods (less often)

After their outer seed coats are removed, broad beans can be eaten
raw, or you can invite them to jump into a cooking pot.

Broad bean - *Vicia faba*

For seven thousand years I have been sown
Across the world, and by these names I'm known:
As *Vicia faba*, broad or fava bean.
I'm full of carbohydrate and protein.

Like all legumes I nourish where I grow,
Catch nitrogen to feed the soil below.
I cope with altitude and with heat too;
I might be growing in a field near you.

The pop of colour as I leave my skin
Means after winter, spring is coming in
When loudly sings cuckoo in hedgerow fair,
And birds all serenade the warming air.

And if you miss the spring and summer crop
You'll find me waiting in your local shop.
Look for me frozen, dried, canned; in this way
I'll sweeten and sustain you every day.

Broad Bean

Botanical name
Vicia faba L.

Common names
broad bean, fava bean

Origin and native distribution
Middle East

Parts used
seeds, unripe pods (less often)

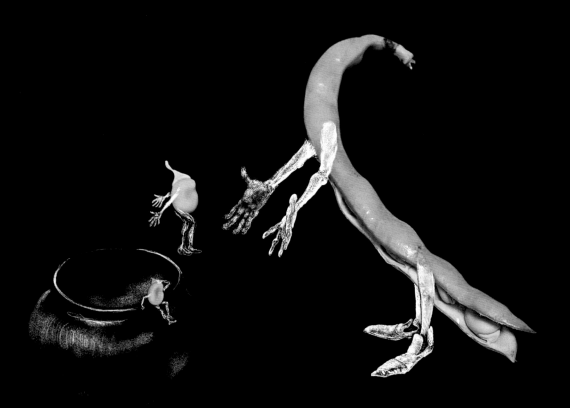

When broad beans are very young their whole seed pod
is tender enough to be eaten whole, and these two escaped seeds
don't need to be shelled before cooking.

Vicia faba, broad beans or fava beans, are an ancient crop that has been sustaining humans and animals since at least 5000 BCE. Remains of cultivated broad beans have been found in the city of Jericho, one of the earliest permanent human settlements. As an easy crop to grow, tolerant of altitude and heat and thriving in temperate climates, they soon spread from the Fertile Crescent of the Middle East to Europe, Africa and Asia. By 1200 CE they were established in China, where today the most broad beans are grown, followed by Ethiopia and Egypt. Broad beans were the only beans known in Europe until Christopher Columbus brought other species back from his voyage to the Americas in 1492.

The majority of broad beans grown today are used for animal feed, but millions of humans also continue the long tradition of enjoying them. As the seeds can be eaten fresh, frozen, dried and ground into flour, they are a reliable and nutritious staple all year round. The beans are high in protein and, being easy to cultivate, were a sensible plant to grow throughout history for people who couldn't often afford to buy meat. Broad beans are also high in phosphorous, which supports the healthy growth of bones and teeth, making them an excellent food from infancy to the grave. They are also credited with the ability to cure warts; rubbing the green seed pods onto the affected skin was a common household remedy.

There is one risk to eating broad beans, but it is quite rare. *Favism* affects a small number of people, usually children with Mediterranean or Middle Eastern heritage. Caused by an enzyme deficiency, this is an allergic reaction to the beans which can cause anaemia.

There are several varieties of broad beans, and the seeds can be eaten at different stages of maturity. When young, the whole seed pod can be consumed, and the individual seeds can be eaten raw with the skins on. When mature, the seed coat becomes tougher and this is often removed after cooking. The mature seeds can be dried, ground into flour, and used in a variety of ways. In Asia and Indonesia, the dried seeds are made into miso and tofu or fermented into soy sauce and tempeh. Fermented broad beans are an important ingredient in Szechuan chilli paste. In Mexico, the dried and peeled seeds are an important ingredient in Sopa de habas, and are also roasted and salted as a snack. The leaves can also be used as a potherb.

The small brown variety of broad beans is the star of the classic Egyptian and Middle Eastern dish ful medames, often eaten for breakfast. The beans are cooked with cumin, lemon juice, garlic, and other spices and herbs such as fresh parsley. The recipe varies across different regions, and the beans can be kept whole or minced into a thick paste.

Blackcurrant, redcurrant and gooseberry

Botanical (and common) names
Ribes nigrum L. (blackcurrant)
Ribes rubrum L. (redcurrant)
Ribes uva-crispa L. (gooseberry)

Origin and native distribution
Europe, Asia
Parts used
fruits

Top: The sour-sharp fruits of blackcurrant and redcurrant.
Bottom: Tart-sweet green gooseberry and the sweeter
claret-coloured red gooseberry admiring the translucent
whitecurrant, a cultivated variety of redcurrant.

Blackcurrant & birds - *Ribes nigrum*

Follow the purpled garden path,
See where the birds have feasted and scattered.
There before you, always, always.
Bright shit announces their *droigt de seigneur*,
Beaks piercing shining black berries in plenty,
Swallowed between songs, joyful in claiming.
All their disdain for your planting and planning -
Tight rows of jam jars, heavy and labelled -
Declared in their royal purple marks on the stone.
Fool to believe any plant is your own.

Blackcurrant & us - *Ribes nigrum*

This challenge I set you, a sharp line to walk,
And too sharp for many to hold their course,
For you boast of my vitamin C; cut it with sugar.
Announce antioxidants; blunt them in processing.
Timid and tongue-shy of my true bold flavour
You sweeten and soften, yet expect power to linger.
Ribes nigrum, watered down for the children;
A spoonful of sugar won't harm that which heals
But the sand dunes of sugar I'm squashed with? Excessive.
Let small faces pucker and scrunch with the sourness,
Or serve with a strawberry to keep smiles intact.
As age weighs more heavily, always advancing,
These leaves, seeds and skin serve to eat and to ease.
In mead and in medicine, sip me at need.
I smooth wrinkles, soothe stomachs, and cure your sore throat.

The small but potent fruits of the *Ribes* family are distinguished by their tartness, high vitamin C content, jewel-like colours and translucent flesh.

Blackcurrant - *Ribes nigrum*

Cultivation of blackcurrants was made illegal in the USA in 1911 when it was discovered that this family can harbour a disease that damages native white pine trees. Recent cures to the disease have allowed blackcurrants to be reintroduced.

Blackcurrants are extremely high in vitamin C, one of the richest known sources providing 70 to 180 milligrams per 100 grams, but the fruit's popularity in the UK has been displaced by the promotion of blueberries. The medicinal properties of blackcurrant have been recognised and used for centuries. It was known as quinsyberry in medieval England and used as a remedy for colds throughout Europe. The fruit's deep colour comes from anthocyanin pigments, which are anti-inflammatory. They are high in other antioxidant phenolic compounds which also counteract bacterial activity, including that of *E. coli*. Blackcurrants are therefore effective against sore throats, colds and stomach bugs. Dried powdered blackcurrant skins are used as a remedy for diarrhoea in Scandinavia.

Blackcurrants can be served with meat but their most common use is in jams, desserts, confectionery and sweet drinks, including the French liqueur crème de cassis and English black mead, a honey wine. A flavoursome tisane can be made from the dried leaves, while fresh leaves can be used in soups. In Belarus, they are used to flavour pickled cucumbers, apples and tomatoes. The flower buds are also eaten in ice cream and used in the production of liqueurs.

Blackcurrant cordial or squash is a popular children's drink which contains huge amounts of sugar, and recently artificial sweeteners too, to counteract the tart flavour. Unfortunately, this inhibits the absorption of vitamin C and counteracts the anti-inflammatory, immune-boosting benefits of the fruit. The adverts and labels don't mention this nutritional conflict.

Blackcurrant's characteristic bitterness, astringency, and intensity of taste are due to the presence of compounds whose exact composition has not yet been fully explained by science. These bioactive compounds and their potential for assisting human health are still being explored. It is clear that blackcurrants can help regulate blood sugar, reduce inflammation, minimise the appearance of wrinkles on the skin, treat eye diseases such as glaucoma, and help athletes' recovery times. Eating the fresh berries, or using them in simple cookery and remedies, gets these beneficial fruits straight into our digestive system for use by the body. Many intensive mechanical and chemical processing and extraction methods deplete the fruit's innate benefits while packaging them into a standardised medicinal or supplement form.

Redcurrant - *Ribes rubrum*

Redcurrants grow in hanging clusters and have a jewel-like glow; they have been called garnetberries. They are expensive to harvest as they must be picked by hand. Whitecurrants are the same plant expressing albino genes. The clarity of the redcurrant's colour makes it an excellent fruit for translucent jellies and jams. To make the French confiture de Bar-le-Duc or compote de luxe, the tiny seeds of redcurrants (or whitecurrants) are individually removed using a goose feather quill, keeping the currants whole and mixing them with sugar syrup. Redcurrant jelly is often paired with turkey, and is an ingredient in Cumberland sauce for meat. Redcurrant juice gives colour to red mead, a form of honey wine or melomel, and redcurrant wine is traditionally served with cherry pie.

Gooseberry - *Ribes uva-crispa*

Gooseberries are appreciated for their crisp texture, tart-sweet taste, and the glossy translucence of their flesh through which the veins are visible. The skin, sparsely covered with hair, is commonly green, but some cultivars are yellow, red or purple. The fruits have been cultivated since the 15th century, and Germany is a major producer. In England there was a flurry of competitive activity around the plant. Gooseberry Clubs began in Manchester in the 1840s and extended through the surrounding regions, with prizes given to the finest and largest fruits. Selective growing for competition increased the size of gooseberries nationwide.

A classic dish is gooseberry fool, a sweetened puree of the fruits served with whipped cream. The fruits are also eaten raw, used in jams, jellies, chutneys, relishes, pies and desserts, and made into wine. In France the fruits are used almost exclusively to make sauce to accompany oily fish, traditionally mackerel, hence their common name groseille à maquereau.

The Frankish word *krûsil*, meaning *crisp berry*, is the origin of the French *groseille*, along with the old English versions *grosier* and *grozer*, which eventually became *gooseberry*; nothing to do with geese at all. The use of gooseberry juice as an anti-inflammatory in traditional medicine led to it being listed in the 1931 book *A Modern Herbal* by Grieve, with names including feverberry, and the evocative goosegogs and honeyblobs.

Walnut

Juglandaceae family

Botanical name
Juglans regia L.

Common names
common walnut, Persian walnut

Origin and native distribution
Central Asia

Parts used
seeds

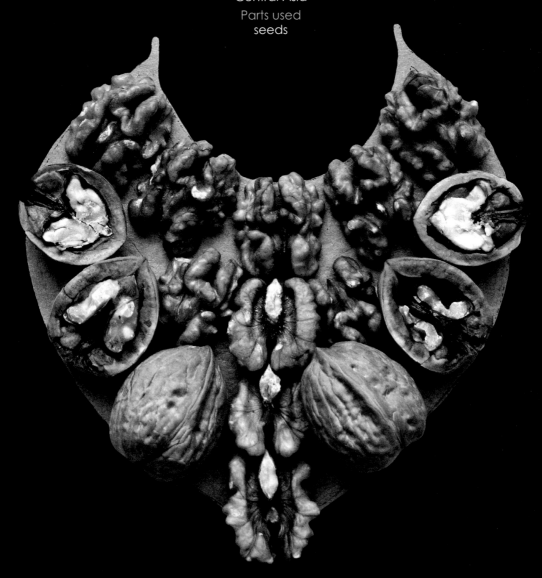

The opened walnut shells above reveal the wrinkled,
brain-like kernels inside. Walnuts are one of the most popular nuts in the
Western world, and different cultivars vary in size and shape.

Walnut - *Juglans regia*

The old gods are not well worshipped these days.
Juno, Mars, Venus, Bacchus, Jove.
Acts of love, war, and excess run their course
Without ritual, without clear intent.
Jove as the father of gods, the all-mighty,
What offerings are set before him now?
Before you bring the oxen or goat,
The knife and the flame, the bowl for the entrails,
Remember that strength is not wedded to size.

I'll stain your ground as well as blood.
I'll dye your hair as deep as henna.
I'll oil your skin and drench your leaves.
I'll crumble; but don't you doubt my taste.
I stand up to coffee, to stilton's bite.
I breathe bitterness, I will stay and fight.

Clacking sackfuls of nuts, let them scatter.
Jove has the power to crack each one wide,
Revealing two hemispheres, wrinkled brown.
Tender, they resemble the mind of man.

Bodies are altars awaiting the flame;
Creation, the thunderbolt, raw, untamed.
Deep furrows cleave the philosopher's brow.
Whose flesh will bear witness to Jove's power now?

The walnut is so popular that in many European countries the word for *nut* is also the word for *walnut*. Its common name tells us it's a traveller; *walnut* comes from the Old English word *wealhhnutu*, meaning *foreign nut*. The Romans brought it from Persia and distributed it across their Empire from Europe to North Africa. Later, it was carried along the Silk Roads to China, and across the Atlantic Ocean to America.

The Latin name, *Juglans regia*, claims the nut for Jupiter or Jove, king of the Roman gods. *Juglans (walnut)* combines the *ju* of Jupiter with *glans*, meaning *acorn*, so the walnut is Jupiter's acorn, and *regia* means *royal*. Jupiter lived on walnuts when he came to earth; no other nut would do. They are literally food for the king of the gods.

Juglans regia trees can grow up to 30 metres tall, and their beautiful wavy-grained wood is highly prized for making furniture, gun stocks, musical instruments, car interiors, and in wood carving and decorative arts.

The wrinkled shell of the walnut has two lobes joined by a ridge or seam, which separate into two "boats" that float on water. Inside this hard exterior is one of the softest of all nuts. Their deeply wrinkled, brain-like shape helps them crumble into pieces in the hand. Walnuts have a grown-up taste: strong, slightly bitter, with a depth that marries well with the robust flavours of coffee and gorgonzola cheese, and contrasts with the sweetness of dates.

As walnuts are high in omega-3 and vitamins E, B and D they are a nutritious snack, but the oil content means they can quickly turn rancid, and they keep best when stored in a cold dark place. The nuts are eaten raw, cooked, in sauces, in baking and confectionery, and yield an oil used to dress salads. Immature green walnuts are pickled in vinegar, preserved in syrup, or made into liqueurs.

The resemblance of walnuts to the two lobes of the brain led to the ancient belief that they had a positive effect on its illnesses. Recent studies suggest that walnuts can indeed improve the memory and brain function thanks to their combination of vitamins, fats and other nutrients.

The walnut in its shell grows within a green husk which, along with the leaves, is used to give a rich red-yellow or brown dye. Ancient Greek women used it to dye their hair; it is also used to colour fabrics and wood floors. When gathering and preparing walnuts be sure to wear gloves.

Brazil nut

Botanical name
Bertholletia excelsa Bonpl.

Common names
Brazil nut, para nut

Origin and native distribution
South America

Parts used
seeds

The distinctive ridged shapes of Brazil nut shells, like orange
segments. The large creamy kernels are held securely inside their
shells that can be tough to crack.

Brazil nut - *Bertholletia excelsa*

You humans are such hungry apes,
It's for my seeds you've come.
Three-sided, creamy, crunchy shapes
Rich in selenium.
Bertholletia excelsa,
Deep in the Amazon
I gaze down to that great river;
I've grown here ages long.

Fruits hard and heavy at the crown
Of trees that tower high
Bring danger as they plummet down;
Be wary of this sky.
The harvesters must carry shields
To keep their skulls intact.
You need your armour on to stroll
Through my woods, that's a fact.

A rustle in the undergrowth;
This friendly agouti
With gnawing teeth will do the most
To set my harvest free.
He gathers seeds to hoard and hide,
But some of them will grow.
By spreading me so far and wide
He helps the forest flow.

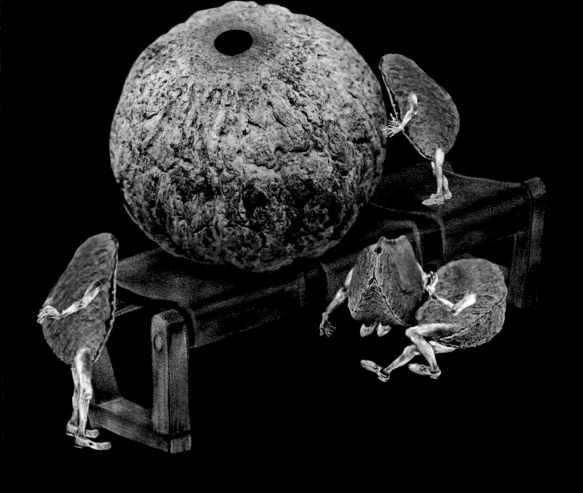

Brazil nut fruit capsules resemble cannonballs, and can
remain unbroken even after falling from trees 50 metres high. Inside
the capsules the seeds are crowded together, each in its shell.

Bertholletia excelsia trees are native to the Amazon region of South America: Brazil, Peru and Bolivia. For the indigenous peoples they have always been a food source, and they have become a major commercial export. Unlike many important crops they have not been cultivated separately, but are harvested primarily from wild forest trees. This promotes conservation. The areas where Brazils flourish are known as *castanhais* in Brazil and *manchales* in Peru.

What we call Brazil nuts are really seeds, which grow together in a perilously hard and heavy ball-shaped fruit capsule. The trees can grow 30 to 50 metres high, and the capsules weigh around 2.5 kilograms, so a falling capsule full of seeds can hit like a cannonball and there are several deaths each year as a result. When harvesting the fallen capsules, people carry shields to protect their skulls.

There can be up to 24 seeds inside each capsule, pressed against one another like seeds in a pomegranate or segments in an orange. This pressure produces their three-sided crescent moon shape, each inside its own hard shell. Brazils are truly formidable, but rodents called agoutis have sharp enough teeth to get into the capsules (humans have to use a machete). As they hoard the seeds around the forest, those which do not get eaten can germinate and produce new trees.

Brazils are notable for providing the highest levels of selenium of any food; this nutrient helps prevent cancer, but should only be eaten in moderation. The seeds are also rich in thiamin (vitamin B1), and contain around 16% protein and 70% oil, making them a high-energy food. They have also been shown to help prevent heart diseases such as atherosclerosis, and assist in managing other health conditions related to obesity and inflammation. Only a small quantity of nuts is needed to make a measurable difference.

Brazil nuts are eaten raw, roasted, salted, coated in chocolate, and used in confectionery. They are used to make savoury sauces and ground into flour for baking or mixed with other flours such as cassava. Brazil nut oil is used in cooking, and in cosmetics.

Lythraceae family

Pomegranate

Botanical name
Punica granatum L.

Common name
pomegranate

Origin and native distribution
Middle East to Southwest Asia

Parts used
fruits (arils), seeds

Whole pomegranate fruits and a bowl filled with the edible seeds,
which are surrounded by juicy, glossy red arils that gleam like jewels.

Pomegranate - *Punica granatum*

A cupful of rubies,
A cupful of juice,
Garnet-deep mysteries;
Beauty and truth
And the knowledge that
Cracked the world's innocence wide,
Spilling seeds like red tears
That no fig leaf could hide.

The fall from high Eden;
And before that tale,
In the Underworld
Persephone was in jail.
Each seed was a month,
A hunger admitted.
The years have their seasons
For acts she committed.

But unreasonable,
Don't you think? Don't you feel
That such trick-playing deities
Lack your urge to heal?
You feed those in hunger.
You clothe those who shiver.
Your helping hands pull
Souls from suffering's river.

So cut back my leather;
This dull rind holds gems,
An abundance to share
With all strangers and friends.
The crown that I wear
Is not only for kings;
It tells you to treasure
Each seed that life brings.

Wild pomegranates probably originated in Persia, modern-day Iran, which is still considered to produce the best varieties. Pomegranates are now found growing across the warm regions from North Africa and Spain through Turkey and the Middle East into China. The shrub or tree can grow up to five metres tall, producing bright orange or red flowers followed by the yellow-red leathery-skinned fruits, topped with an upright calyx like a crown.

Pomegranates were one of the first fruits to be cultivated in the Fertile Crescent of the Middle East, after grain farming had been established around 10,000 years ago. The white seeds are surrounded by an edible aril; juicy red-pink dodecahedrons (twelve-sided). Each fruit contains from around 200 to 1,000 seeds; the word *pomegranate* translates as *apple with many seed grains*.

The Romans sourced the fruits from Carthage, which they called Punica, hence the botanical name *Punica granatum*, with *granatum* meaning *seeds*. The fruit lends its name to the city of Granada in Spain, and also to the hand grenade. Pomegranates are planted deep in mythology and art. They are used in the architecture and folk traditions of the Middle East to represent fertility and hope. The pomegranate features in the Greek myths, and is sometimes claimed as the fruit of the Tree of Knowledge in the Biblical Garden of Eden.

Thanks to its crown-like calyx, the pomegranate was adopted as a symbol of royalty in the Middle Ages. When the Spanish princess Catherine of Aragon married Henry VIII of England, pomegranates and roses were part of the celebrations to represent the two nations. Despite the unhappy end to that union, pomegranate and rose remain a delicious, aromatic and romantic combination in food, drink, and cosmetics.

Pomegranate seeds are eaten raw, used in cooking, pressed for juice, and dried to give a sweet-sour spice anardana, used in Indian and Persian cuisine. The flesh (or arils) has a refreshing sharp-sweet taste, and contains more polyphenol antioxidants than blueberries and citrus fruits. The juice is boiled down into pomegranate molasses, an important ingredient in Middle Eastern and Mediterranean cuisine. The juice is also fermented or mixed with sugar syrup to make grenadine, but many products now sold as grenadine are synthetic, not made from the natural fruits. Pomegranate juice mixed with snow or ice was the historical origin of sherbet. You could add a few drops of rosewater for a breath of summer in the cold months.

All parts of the plant have long-standing uses in traditional medicine, and pomegranate extract shows potential for treating certain cancers. The leathery rind and the tree bark are used for tanning leather and producing dyes.

Malvaceae family
Okra

Botanical name
Abelmoschus esculentus (L.) Moench

Common names
okra, gumbo, lady's finger, bhindi

Origin and native distribution
Tropical Africa, Tropical Asia

Parts used
young fruits, young leaves,
flowers, seeds

Two cultivated varieties of the immature fruits of okra, showing
their star shape in cross-section slices. The African variety is short and
squat, and the Asian variety is more long and thin.

Okra - *Abelmoschus esculentus*

Grasp these slippery, slimy fingers:
Their taste is mild; the texture lingers.
You won't forget our touch, so tender;
Short squat shapes or long and slender.
Smooth or sometimes slightly hairy,
Our green fruits can alarm unwary
Cooks who find our mucus trying;
It's lessened by baking or frying.

Fresh, dried and ground in Madagascar;
Tajines and foutou of Africa:
There we began but could not remain;
Our journey was born from human pain.
To Southeast USA we travelled
With slaves whose lives had been unravelled.
Transplanted, we began to grow
And nourish all with Creole gumbo.

We thicken the sauce and pepper-pot;
Fruits, seeds and leaves, you can use the lot.
Pick us before we get too tough;
Three or five days old is quite enough.
Lady's finger, bhindi, okra,
Each slice reveals itself a star.
Shining with vitamins A, B, C,
Magnesium, minerals set free.
Your first touch won't unleash our slime,
We'll wait until it's cooking time
When heat releases all our goo.
Come, get this gumbo into you.

Abelmoschus esculentus or okra, gumbo or lady's finger is native to Africa, and is now grown in all the world's subtropical, tropical and warm temperate regions. It is known as *bhindi* in India and *bamyah* in the Middle East, and is related to cotton, hibiscus and roselle. Okra was carried to the Southeastern United States on slave ships and became an important ingredient in Cajun and Creole cuisine. It lends its name to the official cuisine of the state of Louisiana, gumbo, in which a mix of ingredients including vegetables, fish and meat are cooked in a sauce which relies on okra for its mucilaginous texture.

This one-pot style of cooking was popular in Africa, especially West Africa, where the dishes were often known as pepper-pots as they used a lot of chilli peppers as a flavouring. Similar dishes are popular in the Caribbean; like gumbo they show the culinary inheritance of the slave trade and the influence of African cooking.

Okra is an annual herb which grows up to two metres high; the edible fruits are 10 to 20 centimetres long with a slim tapering five-ribbed shape, which when sliced resemble stars. It is important to harvest okra when young, just 3 to 5 days old, as they become tough and hairy as they mature. Okra is an underutilised plant with great potential to solve some culinary dilemmas and to benefit human health. The fruits contain many round seeds and a slimy water-retaining mucilage, which is used in traditional medicine for constipation and as a cooling, soothing cream for the skin. The seeds contain many phytochemicals that are effective anti-diabetic and anti-cancer agents, and they are also active in treating fatigue.

Okra is highly nutritious, rich in magnesium, calcium, phosphorous, potassium, iron and vitamins A, B and C. The glutinous nature of okra makes it an excellent thickener for stews, soups, tajines (North Africa) and foutou (West Africa), but it can be cooked in many ways. It is eaten fresh or dried in Africa and Madagascar, and the leaves and flowers can be cooked as a green vegetable. The leaves can also be dried and powdered. Okra has a mild flavour, and a drier, less slimy texture can be achieved through baking or frying.

The edible seeds have a versatile range of culinary uses. They contain around 20% to 35% protein and a similar level of amino acids as soybeans, so they make an excellent substitute to soybeans for making tofu and tempeh. They are used to make bread rich in fibre and protein, but without the gluten that some people have difficulty digesting. They are ground to make a drink which tastes like coffee but with none of the caffeine; this is already popular in Turkey.

Moraceae family
Breadfruit

Botanical name
Artocarpus altilis (Parkinson) Fosberg
Common names
breadfruit, fruta de pan
Origin and native distribution
Tropical Asia (Indonesia)
Parts used
fruits

A whole, heavy breadfruit with slices of the white, starchy
and fibrous pulp ready for cooking.

Breadfruit - *Artocarpus altilis*

The peace of the Pacific,
The swelling of the waves;
The fury of the mutineers,
The hunger of the slaves.

The late seventeen-hundreds
Were years of slavery.
To feed the stolen people was
The role chosen for me.
Tahiti to Jamaica,
The oceans in between.
Those frightening days upon the waves,
So long with land unseen.

Mutineers on the *Bounty*
Left me adrift, at sea.
My second ship, the *Providence*,
Safely transported me.
Though paradise had grown me
I fed people in hell,
Who missed the life of their homelands
And knew sorrow too well.

My deep-lobed leaves give cool shade
Where villagers can meet.
My large round fruits feed families,
My bounty lines the street.
I hope to feed more nations,
For hunger is a hell.
This earth provides enough for all
And I remember well

The peace of the Pacific,
The swelling of the waves;
The fury of the mutineers,
The hunger of the slaves.

Breadfruit was first spread through the Pacific by voyaging islanders, but its journey to the Caribbean was a result of the horrific demands of the slave trade. When Captain Cook sailed to Tahiti in 1769, botanist and naturalist Joseph Banks accompanied him. The slave trade had resulted in an urgent need to find cheap, sustaining food to keep the slaves alive, and to keep plantations profitable. Banks saw the potential of breadfruit as a suitable crop and, as advisor to King George III, he gained royal support to transport plants from Tahiti to the West Indies.

Unfortunately, the first attempt was under the stewardship of Captain Bligh on the HMS Bounty, and on 28 April 1789 the breadfruit plants were all thrown overboard by the mutineering crew. Both breadfruit and Bligh made a second attempt on the HMS Providence, which reached St Vincent and Jamaica in 1793.

The flesh of the breadfruit is dry, starchy, somewhat fibrous, and also somewhat tasteless. The slaves rejected it, and it was fed to the pigs. Over time, the subtle strengths of the plant became apparent. Breadfruit's mildness makes it versatile; receptive to the flavours of coconut, onion and spices. Its mealy texture has made it a filling staple across the Pacific for 3,000 years, and longer in the Malay archipelago where it was first cultivated. Breadfruit is full of complex carbohydrates that provide energy, is gluten free and contains fibre, essential amino acids and minerals.

As its name suggests, breadfruit's starch content makes it a useful extender of bread flour when it is dried and ground; this is a common use in several African countries. Unripe fruits can be cooked like potatoes: boiled, roasted, baked, fried, steamed, and mashed. Ripe fruits have a sweeter taste and can be eaten raw or fermented. The male flower is eaten as a vegetable; it is the female flower that develops into the breadfruit.

Breadfruit is a generous plant: one tree can provide a year's food security for a family, producing up to 200 fruits in a season. Unlike other Pacific staples such as rice and potatoes, it can be easily grown rather than imported, and requires less labour than other starchy crops like taro or sweet potato. In Samoa, where breadfruit trees provide welcome shade on village streets, it is part of everyday life. On Sundays, smoke rises from earth ovens or *umu* across the islands; breadfruit, often cooked in coconut milk, is an essential part of the *umu* feast. While its traditional role continues in its native Pacific, breadfruit is now being carried once more across the oceans.

Breadfruit is perfectly suited to tackling the nutritional poverty so widespread in tropical and subtropical regions where its plants can thrive, and yet it is not widely grown beyond the fringes of the Pacific Ocean. This is changing, with researchers such as Diane Rangone of The Breadfruit Institute working to conserve and promote traditional breadfruit knowledge and varieties in their native lands, and to introduce the plants into other countries in order to reduce nutritional poverty and deforestation around the world.

Modern horticultural techniques are being combined with the traditional Pacific way of growing breadfruit; not as a monoculture, but alongside other trees and crops. Plants of different heights grow together in agricultural forests or agroforests, providing a year-round variety of foods and contributing to soil health and land regeneration. As breadfruit tolerates a range of conditions, it can thrive across the tropics and provide plentiful food as well as animal fodder and building materials. It is also used medicinally, as the phenolic compounds it contains have antimicrobial effects against pathogenic microorganisms.

Although they are not true fruits, breadfruit and jackfruit belong to the genus *Artocarpus*, a member of the family *Moraceae*, to which breadnut, mulberries and figs belong.

Jackfruit

Botanical name	Origin and native distribution
Artocarpus heterophyllus Lam.	Southwest India, Southern Asia
Common name	Parts used
jackfruit	fruits, seeds

Whole jackfruits with a sliced-open fruit and three segments
of the ripe yellow flesh, whose sweet taste is reminiscent of pineapple
and melon. The seeds are edible when cooked.

Jackfruit - *Artocarpus heterophyllus*

If you are still in childhood,
Not grown to your full height,
I may be taller than you are
When standing straight, upright.

My swelling fruit can grow to
A whole metre in length.
Fifty kilos is quite a weight
To carry - you'll need strength!

Jackfruit is made for sharing,
Even the way it's grown
From flower clusters, not just one;
Too big to eat alone.

My flesh is gold and sunny,
It's eaten cooked or raw,
And as I ripen, so my taste
Will sweeten more and more.

When travelling in Asia
Be careful to where you sit;
A jackfruit falling on your head
Would hurt more than a bit.

The jackfruit tree shoots up quickly, and bears the largest edible tree-fruit. The tree can reach up to 10 metres high and the fruits, which often grow directly on its trunk, can ripen to 60 to 100 centimetres in length. Like the fig and other relatives, the jackfruit develops from flower clusters. Its flesh is made up of hundreds of segments, and each is an individual fruit with a seed surrounded by deep yellow flesh.

In addition to large helpings of food, the jackfruit tree provides fuel, prized timber, and has medicinal uses. It is a useful species for controlling soil erosion as its roots are extensive, and its glossy leaves provide shade for other commercial crops such as cardamom and coffee. The attractive yellow timber resists damage by termites along with fungal and bacterial decay, and it has been used to build palaces and temples. Its heartwood was once used exclusively to make a golden-yellow dye for the robes of Buddhist monks in Southeast Asia; the colour symbolises renouncing desire.

The tree, which is considered indigenous to the western ghats of Southern India, was an ancient cultivated species of Southeast Asia, and has spread to all the world's tropical regions. There are two main types; the fruit of one has a strong smell, a sweet taste, and pulp which is fibrous and mushy. The other type is less strong-smelling, and its flesh is dense and crisp. The jackfruit is not high in energy, having a low carbohydrate content, but is rich in iron, potassium, and nicotinamide, a form of vitamin B3 which nourishes the skin.

When ripe, jackfruit flesh has a sweet taste reminiscent of melon or pineapple. It can be eaten unripe if cooked as a vegetable, and used in curries. When ripe it can be eaten raw along with other fruits, preserved in syrup, made into ice cream, pickled, dried, or fried like chips. Jackfruit has recently become a popular meat substitute in the West, sold canned or used in ready meals or as a pizza topping. The seeds are edible when cooked; like chestnuts they can be roasted, boiled, ground into flour, or fried.

Moraceae family
Fig

Botanical name
Ficus carica L.

Common name
fig

Origin and native distribution
Northern Europe,
Mediterranean region,
Southwest Asia

Parts used
fruits

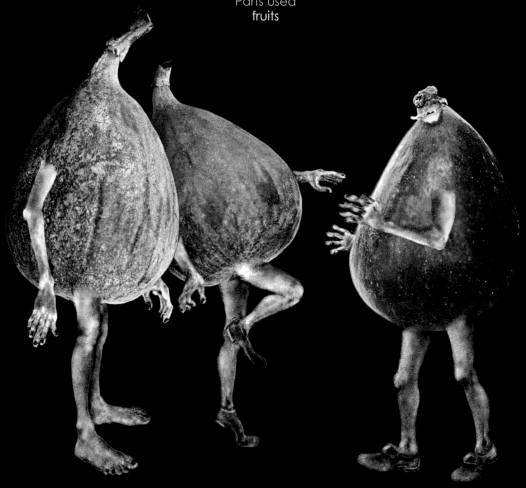

Green and purple cultivated varieties of figs exchanging secrets.
Figs are unique among plants for concealing their flowers
within a fleshy stem called a syconium.

Fig - *Ficus carica*

How did those figs in recent times
Grow by the rivers of Sheffield?
A piece of Eden nourished by
Factory water, from bright steel.

*

Over the hot machines it flowed,
Brought warmth down to the river.
Unlikely Paradise sprang up,
Fig trees began to grow there.

Thanks to the bird that let seeds fall
To warmed earth where they rooted
Sheffield had fig trees, wing-sown, wild;
A miracle had fruited.

Fig's flowers and fruits are kept concealed
Within the skin, a secret.
Then gentle hands reveal our heart;
It's ripe, sweet, delicate.

Heat is the secret to our growth,
Our plants don't like to shiver.
We'll grow in warm and sunny lands
And by the steelwork's river.

A wasteland is unloved, not doomed
To live empty forever.
With care and water it can thrive;
Dirt is not death, remember.

Assuming that all hope is lost
For you or for another
Ignores the miracle of life,
Of warmth, a chance-found mother.

The fig is one of the earliest fruits that humans cultivated. They have been found in excavations of Jericho from the Neolithic level, before pottery was used, pre-dating cereals and legumes. The Egyptians and Mesopotamians cultivated figs around 4000 BCE. Figs are mentioned in the Bible and are one of the contenders for the Tree of Knowledge.

The Romans introduced figs into Britain but only hardy varieties will survive outdoors in the UK, and they are often grown against warm south-facing walls which store the sun's heat. In recent history figs became naturalised in Sheffield on riverbanks close to the steel factories. River water was used as a coolant, and when it was returned to its source, warmed by the machinery, it created an environment in which bird-dropped fig seeds could establish themselves.

Ficus belongs to the *Moraceae*, the same family as the mulberry (*Morus*). *Ficus carica* is closely related to *Ficus religiosa*, the religious or sacred fig tree or bodhi tree under which the Buddha, Gautama Siddhartha, attained enlightenment through meditation. It is also related to *Ficus elastica*, the rubber plant. The latex which can be obtained from figs is used to curdle warm milk for making cheese and junket.

The fig is unique among plants in having a structure called a syconium, which can be thought of as a fleshy stem growing into an inverted flower. The fig's swelling, thin-skinned lobe is hollow, containing many tiny flowers which develop into dry crunchy fruits like seeds. At the base of the fruit there is an ostiole, a little hole, through which small wasps enter to pollinate the plant. There are hundreds of fig cultivars with skin colour varying between green, brown, black and purple, and each one has its specialist species of pollinating wasp. Modern fig cultivars are self-fertile and can be grown from cuttings rather than relying on pollination, enabling them to be grown in regions such as the UK which do not have resident fig wasps.

Drying figs intensifies their nutritional content and also prevents their decay, making them an important historical food for long journeys.

Syrup of figs has been used as a laxative for centuries.

Nelumbonaceae family
Sacred lotus

Botanical name	Origin and native distribution
Nelumbo nucifera Gaertn.	Asia, Australia
Common names	Parts used
sacred lotus, lin ngau	seeds, rhizomes, flowers, leaves

The delicious rhizome of sacred lotus with a halo of slices showing its
distinctive perforations, together with its fresh and dried seeds.

Sacred lotus - *Nelumbo nucifera*

My face raised up each day to light I pray
These roots in river mud might keep me firm,
My purpose pure, my petals shining bright
To guide the minds that seek to understand.

There is no path to glory swept all clear.
Each muddy footstep, each unsettled stone
That trips the pilgrim on their halting way
Adds time for teaching, honesty of heart.

No mud, no lotus; so sings the refrain
Of patient wisdom poured each day anew
To ears that listen to the space within,
While balancing the whirling claims of life.

To bodies hungry for sustaining food
I offer gladly each part of myself.
From roots in mud, these lace-filled rhizomes give
Crisp starch to garnish or to form the meal.

The sealed cup that I bear aloft is full
Of seeds whose strength can last a thousand years.
A bitter kernel hides to be sought out,
Like truths we find acknowledging our pain.

My leaves that spread across the lily pond
And lotus flowers above them, white and red,
Are offerings themselves for your delight
To see, to wish, to taste, to do what's best.

The sacred lotus thrives in the warm muddy waters of tropical regions, and was domesticated in Asia around 7,000 years ago.

The sacred lotus is a culturally and economically important plant, cherished throughout Asia. It has been sacred to India, Tibet and China for centuries and is at the heart of their spiritual traditions. China has been cultivating the sacred lotus for thousands of years and remains one of the world's primary regions for its breeding and cultivation. It is valued for its beauty, and in addition to its practical service as food and medicine it is widely used for ornamentation.

The lotus represents purity and spiritual transformation. "No mud, no lotus" is the teaching that difficulties are fuel for spiritual development, just as the mud of the river bottom nourishes the roots that give rise to the beautiful lotus flower: the mud is necessary. Just as the whole of life is part of the spiritual path, the whole lotus is used by humans. It is a substantial food crop and medicinal uses have also been developed over the years, harnessing the properties of its many bioactive compounds.

Sacred lotus is primarily cultivated for its rhizomes or roots and for its seeds. The rhizomes have an almond-like flavour and are rich in vitamins and minerals. Thanks to the air vessels running through them for buoyancy, when sliced in cross-section lotus root has a lacy or floral pattern. While it appears delicate it remains strong and crunchy.

Young lotus leaves can be stuffed, used to wrap foods, eaten as a vegetable and salad leaf. Lotus flower petals are used as a garnish and floated in soups, and their pollen and stamens are used to perfume tea.

Lotus seeds, often known as nuts, grow in a compound fruit which looks like a sealed cup. They are very nutritious but contain a bitter germ which is usually removed upon harvesting; this is sometimes used to make a herbal tisane. The seeds are also ground for use in Chinese mooncakes eaten at the mid-autumn festival and popular throughout Asia.

The lotus has had to respond to the challenges of growing up from mud, through water, and into air and light. These radically different environments, inhabited simultaneously, have led to the lotus evolving highly creative ways to thrive. The sacred lotus has developed into a triply miraculous plant, exhibiting longevity, thermogenesis and ultrahydrophobicity.

Longevity: if conditions are right the seeds can lie dormant in river mud for a millenium without losing their potential for growth. An ancient peat bog in Manchuria held seeds which were carbon-dated to around 1,000 years old and were still capable of germinating. Scientific research suggests that this remarkable viability is due to an enzyme the seeds produce to repair damaged cells before germination.

Thermogenesis: The lotus flower is unique in its practice of floral organ thermogenesis. The flower generates heat, possibly to entice temperature sensitive pollinators (beetles and other winged insects) which the plant relies on for its reproduction. As well as creating a warm, inviting place for pollinators to visit and linger, the heat may also help to release the volatile compounds which are another attraction for the insects.

Ultrahydrophobicity: this is known as the "lotus effect", whereby the leaves repel water from their self-cleaning surfaces. Research into this action has been used to develop a self-cleaning industrial paint. This quality is another example of lotus' ability to remain pure and let the dirt and pollutants of life slide off, while being nourished by the mud below.

Oxalidaceae family
Bilimbi and starfruit

Botanical name
Averrhoa bilimbi L.

Common name
bilimbi

Origin and native distribution
Tropical Southeast Asia

Parts used
fruits

Botanical name
Averrhoa carambola L.

Common names
starfruit, carambola

Origin and native distribution
Tropical Asia

Parts used
fruits

Here are the unripe green and ripe yellow starfruits holding
their close relative, the sharply acidic bilimbi.

(Loosely based on the poem 'In the beginning' by Dylan Thomas)

Bilimbi and starfruit
- Averrhoa bilimbi and *Averrhoa carambola*

In the beginning was the five-pointed star;
From flowers of five pink petals grew the fruit,
All clustered and hanging down from the branch
Beneath the breeze-blown canopy of leaves,
Awaiting fingers reaching up to claim
Vigour and form raised by the sun.

In the beginning we arose as one
But chose our own courses, a pole each for each.
Bilimbi's smooth green lengths are acid sour;
Impossible raw, but once cooked, a treat.
Bright orange carambola, soft skin unpeeled,
Is star-spiked with slices whose shape points to sweet.

Bilimbi - *Averrhoa bilimbi*

Bilimbi resembles a small yellow-green cucumber, and is so high in oxalic acid that its juice is used to remove rust and stains. In Malaysia it is known as *belimbing asam*, *asam* meaning *sour*; this fruit is too tart to eat raw. It is used as a souring agent in curries, especially the fish curries of Kerala in India. It is also made into relish, pickles and chutneys. When pickled, the fermentation process reduces the oxalic acid. The fruit is sweetened and preserved in jam, as candied fruit and in syrup. The flowers are also used in conserves. *Averrhoa bilimbi* is a common kitchen garden plant thanks to its household usefulness; in addition to its culinary and cleaning properties it is also used as a medicine for fevers and skin ailments.

Starfruit - *Averrhoa carambola*

Starfruit can be quite tart, but some varieties are sweet enough to slice and eat raw. Their Malay name *belimbing manis, manis* meaning *sweet*, emphasises their potential to be eaten out of hand. The striking five-pointed star shape and thin, glossy skin make them an attractive fruit in salads and desserts. They are green when unripe, turning yellow and then orange when ripe. Their flesh and juice are made into drinks and sherbets. The sour types are often cooked with fish or made into pickle, relish and jelly. The flowers are eaten in salads and conserves, and the leaves can also be cooked as a vegetable. This fruit needs careful handling as its thin skin bruises easily.

Due to the high concentration of oxalic acid in both sour and sweet *Averrhoa*, people with renal problems should avoid the two species.

Oca

Botanical name	Origin and native distribution
Oxalis tuberosa Molina	South America (Andes)
Common names	Parts used
oca, New Zealand yam	tubers, leaves, stems

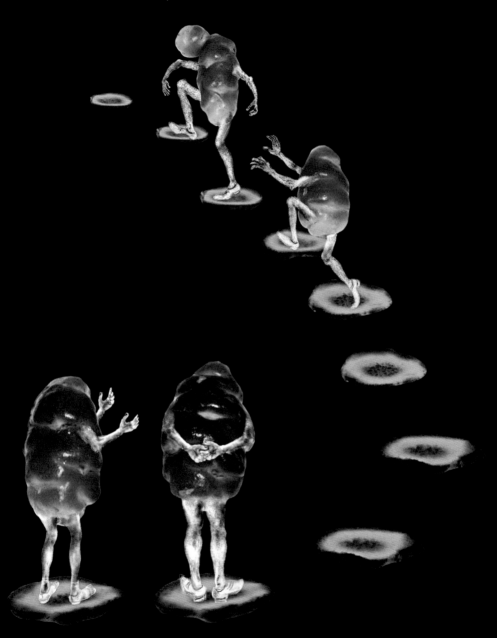

Tubers and slices of pink oca, the high altitude staple that is on the up.

Oca - *Oxalis tuberosa*

When tubers and fruits left my continent's shores
With conquistadors homebound for Spain,
They overlooked me in the Andean hills,
But I'm not here to whine or complain.
It suits me quite well to remain with my folks
Who have eaten me for centuries,
Though spotlights in future may shine on my skin:
A new culinary trend, starring me.

You've heard of potatoes? We're not really linked
But you wouldn't think that from our looks.
My white, red and yellow lumps, tubers of starch,
Could replace them in recipe books.
When vertigo strikes and potatoes climb down
To their fields at the foot of the hills,
It's me that continues and flourishes high
In the mountains, the world's windowsills.

At first I taste bitter; *oxalis* is Greek
For the acid my raw state provides.
But left out to dry in the sun for a week
I mellow and show my sweet side.
From then on I cook like potatoes, except
That sometimes I am safe to eat raw.
As oca I'm sold as the tuberous crop
That only potatoes outscore.

Oca is found growing in all seven countries of the Andes, which travel the west coast of South America and form the longest mountain range on earth. It is resistant to frost, tolerant of drought and poor soils, and can be grown at high altitude. So why did oca, the second most cultivated tuber after potatoes in Peru and Bolivia, not spread throughout Europe along with potatoes and tomatoes? The answer lies in the tubers.

Tubers are the plant's energy storage system. They are ideal for sustaining human communities through winter months, providing carbohydrates, protein, calcium and iron. Tubers left in the ground can also produce buds that grow into new tubers; an affordable, nutritious, low-effort highland crop.

However, to form tubers below ground the plant requires short days with 9 hours of sunlight. Longer days with 13 hours of light lead to more vegetation above ground. This has kept it rooted in its ancient Inca lands; close enough to the equator to receive consistent sunlight and high enough to temper this with cool and cloudy weather. It has also been introduced to New Zealand where it is known as New Zealand yam.

When oca tubers are dried in the sun for 6 to 10 days they can almost double in sugar content. Sour types of oca contain oxalic acid, named after the Greek word for *acid*, *oxalis*. The acid breaks down with exposure to the sun, and the oca's flavour and texture is transformed into something closer to carrot and sweet potato with lemony notes; it can be eaten raw or cooked. The sweetened tubers become dry, floury and wrinkled. While improving the flavour, the release of sugars makes sunned oca more susceptible to mould and decay, especially in warmer climates. The leaves can be eaten as salad and the acidic stems can be cooked like rhubarb.

Wild potatoes also prefer a short day, but this tendency has been bred out; so with skilful cultivation there is potential for oca to join potatoes on tables worldwide, all year round.

Breadseed poppy

Botanical name
Papaver somniferum L.
Common names
breadseed poppy, opium poppy
Origin and native distribution
West Asia, Mediterranean region
Parts used
seeds

Black poppy seeds are the most well known in the
Western world, used on cakes and breads, while in Asian
cooking the white form is more widely used.

Breadseed poppy - *Papaver somniferum*

"To sleep, perchance to dream"*; I've led
Many an artist to their bed
Where fantasy, that sweet escape,
Returns in poesy when they wake.

I'm *Papaver somniferum*,
Sleep bearing, restful as the tomb.
My analgesic opium
From latex flows, to calm the storm.

I hope you'll never call on me
For morphine; that you'll live long, free
From suffering; but know me through
My tiny seeds that nourish you.

In Europe black, in Asia white,
For bread and cakes and salads bright,
Pressed into oil or crushed and spread;
Shake countless seeds from my cupped head.

Another poppy, *rhoeas*,
Grows over soldiers; through the grass
Their red recalls how blood was lost
Protecting freedom, at great cost.

Whenever poppies meet your eye,
Red, gold, white, orange, just think why
One slender bloom should take such strain;
Mourning the dead, masking our pain.

* from *Hamlet* by William Shakespeare

The tiny seeds of *Papaver somniferum*, or opium poppy, are held in distinctive flat-topped, cup-shaped heads. Holes in the top allow the seeds to be shaken out and dispersed by the wind or collected by humans. The plant was cultivated by the ancient Sumerians, and in addition to the edible seeds it has powerful medical uses.

Before they mature, the green seed capsules are a source of a latex called opium. This is a potent mix of alkaloid drugs including morphine, heroin and codeine, which reduce pain and induce sleep or a dream-like state. The seeds do not have soporific or mind-altering effects so they are commonly and safely eaten.

Seed colour can vary from white, yellow, and grey, to bluish black, and this variation affects the oil and protein content. Oils can turn rancid over time, especially in warm conditions, so the seeds are best stored in an airtight container in the fridge. Asian poppy seeds are white. The European black seeds can have a blue tint, which is an optical illusion caused by the refraction of light on tiny calcium oxalate crystals; these cause blue light to be reflected. Dutch poppy seeds are prized for their attractive slate blue colour.

During the Opium Wars of the 1830s to 1860s, opium's history became bound up with that of tea. To fund their taste for this beverage, the British were growing opium in their colonies and selling it in China. The drug was addictive and harmful to health, so the Chinese government tried to stop its sale. The British responded by establishing rival tea plantations in their colonies in India, and this grew into a huge industry.

Whole poppy seeds are used in breads and baked goods, salads, and in savoury dishes. They are popular in German and Eastern European baking. They can be crushed and sweetened to make a filling for pastries and crêpes. In Asia, white poppy seeds are fried and ground into a paste, adding thickness to curries along with a nutty flavour. In Turkey a paste is made from the oil mixed with roasted, ground seeds. Half the weight of poppy seeds comes from their oil, and this oil, known as olivette, is widely used in French cooking.

Poppy seed oil is also used in soaps, paints and varnishes, and the seeds are included in bird feed mixes.

Stone pine nut and Korean pine nut

Botanical name	Botanical name
Pinus pinea L.	*Pinus koraiensis* Siebold and Zucc.

Common names
umbrella pine, Italian stone
or pesto pine, pignolia nut

Common names
Korean pine nut,
Chinese pine nut

Origin and native distribution
Mediterranean region

Origin and native distribution
Eastern Asia

Parts used
seeds

Parts used
seeds

Long, slender Italian stone pine seeds and the stout,
egg-shaped Korean pine nuts. Delicious little flavour bombs;
opinions differ as to which cultivar is best, and prices vary.

Stone pine nut - *Pinus pinea*

Pinus pinea fringing coastlines and foothills
Of Mediterranean lands in the sun.
Along Roman roads and in Renaissance gardens
My tall trunks provide welcome structure and shade.

Undo the cones, in whose shapely protection
Sweet resinous seeds have matured for three years.
If you have the time, let the sun do the work
As my scales open up to the warmth in the air.

My spreading umbrella of needle-like leaves
Makes tisane to revive the mind and senses.
The Romans stuffed dormice with creamy-sweet seeds
And served them at special occasions and feasts.

Korean pine nut - *Pinus koraiensis*

Korea and China use me in abundance,
My seeds raw or roasted; but more of me too.
My pollen gives flavour to Korean cookies,
And cones breathe their fragrant green scent into wine.

China sends sackfuls of pine nuts away
Into other lands keen for a taste of this tree.
With even more oil than my *pinea* kin,
Koraiensis is one seed worth searching for.

Added to candies and sticky rice puddings,
Ground into powder to coat a sweet cake
Or in savoury dishes, salted or fried,
My small tasty seeds have their part to play.

The stone pine is native to the coastal regions of Mediterranean Europe, growing on hills and the lower slopes of mountains as well as on dunes and well-drained flat ground. It has been cultivated for its tiny, high-energy nuts for over 6,000 years, and wild-harvested long before that. Pine nuts were an important source of protein during the Palaeolithic era and for later hunter-gatherers. The tree usually has a lifespan of around 150 years but can live to be 300 years old. The striking shape of the pine cone has featured in works of art from ancient times and has also been a focus of spiritual devotion.

Both male and female cones are produced on the same tree. The male cones give pollen and the female cones give pine nuts, which take three years to mature. Pine nuts are botanically categorised as seeds, as they are held inside the cones but not fully encased. In hot weather the cones open up and release their seeds, which are then eaten by birds and rodents, helping to disperse the species.

Humans harvest the ripe cones which are then sun-dried and threshed or cracked by rollers to release the seeds. These are then hulled, usually by machine, to remove the hard shell so that the cream or pale brown kernel is sold ready for culinary use. This labour-intensive process makes the finished product expensive to buy. Their high oil content means they can quickly turn rancid, so it is best to buy them in small quantities and keep them frozen to prevent waste.

The resinous turpentine flavour and crunchy texture of the pine nut makes it a small but potent source of interest in dishes such as salads and pilafs. Varieties range from 1.5 to 2 centimetres long, with a shape that can be almost cylindrical or more tapering and egg-shaped. Toasting increases the flavour as the heat releases volatile oils. Pine nuts are famous for their use in pesto, pounded with basil, garlic, olive oil, lemon juice and hard cheese (usually pecorino). They are also used in cakes, stuffings, sweetmeats, desserts and cookies, and in dolmas (stuffed vine leaves). In Portugal they are sugar-coated at Easter in the same way as almonds. In Roman times they were used to stuff dormice as a delicacy for the wealthy.

Once empty, pine cones make useful fuel for fires. The trees have also been used for wood, including shipbuilding. Stone pines are often known as umbrella pines for their attractive spreading shape and valuable shade. They were planted along Roman roads such as the Via Appia, and in the ornamental gardens of the Italian Renaissance. During the Ottoman period the hills of the Bosphorus Strait in Istanbul were also planted with shapely stone pines. They are now cultivated for soil conservation, to protect coastal dunes from erosion, and to benefit the agricultural crops of the coastal Mediterranean.

Other related pine trees are also harvested to a lesser extent. Related species grow around the Mediterranean and others are found in Asia, Southwestern USA and Mexico.

China is a major exporter of the seeds of *Pinus koraiensis*, which have a higher oil content than those of American and European pines. As well as being eaten raw or roasted, the seeds are used in candies, cakes, kimchi, glutinous rice desserts, and meat dishes such as a kind of steak tartare. Fried seeds are used to garnish savoury dishes and also drinks. In Korea, the green cones are used in wine making and the pollen is gathered for making cookies. Pine nut powder is popular in Korea: the seeds are ground or finely chopped and the powder is sprinkled over foods such as sweet rice cakes.

Black pepper

Botanical name
Piper nigrum L.

Common name
black pepper

Origin and native distribution
Southwest India

Parts used
fruits

Fresh green pepper spike shown with black, white and
powdered peppercorns, all from the same plant. Different picking times
and processing methods produce the range of colours and flavours.

Black pepper - *Piper nigrum*

Rain is my secret, the magic of birth.
Petrichor's sweetness; the scent of the earth
Once rain has come; life returns, and relief
Is sipped into stalk, flower, berry and leaf.
On Malabar's coast I creep up shade trees,
Winding my vines to enjoy the warm breeze.
On sharp stalks my berry clusters grow green,
Picked at the first glimpse of red that is seen,
Or left to ripen as pungency fades,
Dwindling as berries glow red in green shades.

Day after day after sweet rainy day
Water feeds fire, the alchemical way.

The king of spice, I'm worth my weight in gold -
That's no turn of phrase - history has told
How scales measured shrivelled circles of black
Against gleaming gold coins, and found no lack.
For centuries, debts of trade or of land
Would be settled with my hot spheres in hand.
Pepper was power: just like that resource
Too much is unwise, to share's the best course,
As wealth held too tightly stops love flowing,
Constricts the channels where friendship's growing.

Day after day after sweet rainy day
Water feeds fire, the alchemical way.

Piper nigrum, black pepper, also known as the king of spices, is one of the oldest and most widely used spices in the world. It has been cultivated for at least 4,000 years. The insistent heat and aromatic pungency of pepper are still highly prized, and today around 30% of the world's spice trade is in black pepper.

Piper nigrum is native to the Malabar coast of Southwest India. To grow well it requires tropical temperatures, partial shade, and a long rainy season. The plant is a perennial woody climber, which puts forth many slender hanging clusters of flowers. These flower "spikes" are followed by the small round fruits or "drupes" which we know as peppercorns.

Today pepper is cultivated in tropical lands, including countries in South America and Africa, with India, Indonesia, Vietnam and Brazil as the leading producers. The Malabar coast is still the source of the most high-status and strongly aromatic Tellicherry and Malabar berries. Each growing region produces different varieties: the Malabar coast alone has over 75 varieties or hybrids. Each variety has its own characteristic balance of volatile oils which affect the flavour, heat and pungency you experience when you add pepper to your food.

Black, white, red and green peppercorns are sold as distinct products but all come from the same plant. Different harvesting times and processing methods produce the four colours. Green peppercorns are harvested unripe, and pickled to maintain their green colour. Red are harvested when ripe, and then dried, which turns the red skin a deep maroon. White are harvested ripe, then soaked, dried, and the red skin removed. Black are picked just before ripeness, when the lowest fruits on the hanging spike are just turning red. The best black pepper is fermented overnight and sun-dried, but sometimes the berries are blanched before being dried. Pink pepper is not from the same plant, it belongs to the mango family, and Szechuan pepper is not from the same family either.

Until the 4th century BCE, black pepper stayed close to home. For centuries it was the original hot and spicy ingredient of Indian and Asian food. In 327 BCE, Alexander the Great invaded India and discovered a wealth of spices too good to leave behind. This changed the course of European history and cookery, and established black pepper as a distinguishing mark of fine cuisine. Pepper became a kind of black gold. The costs of transportation from India and the rivalry in Europe to control its distribution made it an expensive status symbol for centuries. When Rome was under siege in 408 CE at the hands of Attila the Hun, he demanded 3,000 pounds of peppercorns (equivalent to over a ton) as part of the city's ransom. In Europe in the Middle Ages peppercorns were literally worth their weight in gold and were traded ounce for ounce.

The desire for pepper at an affordable price, and the sudden prospect of the supply being stopped, were the catalysts for the Age of Exploration. When the Ottoman Empire (modern-day Turkey) decided to stop trading with the West in 1453, they closed the traditional overland route between Europe and the Middle East. Europe's seafaring nations now raced towards the source of pepper in India. In 1498 Vasco da Gama from Portugal discovered a sea route to Southwest India, and this gave Portugal control over the valuable pepper exports for many years.

In 1492, Christopher Columbus from Spain had also sailed in search of pepper. He ended up not in India but in the Americas, the New World. Not realising his mistake he referred to the native people as Indians.

When pepper sits quietly next to salt on the table it is easy to consider it as merely a condiment, a little extra to the meal, but it is also an essential ingredient that brings its flavour and pungent, aromatic heat to the cuisine of almost every country in the world.

In its native India, black pepper is an important component of garam masala and other blends. It was Arabic people who first traded pepper in Europe, so it is not surprising that it features in their spice mixtures such as zhoug and baharat. In France it is one of the quatre épices: black pepper, cloves, nutmeg and dried ginger. It gives its name to poivrade sauce, pfefferkuchen, pepper steak, and pepato cheese.

Pepper's flavour mellows during cooking, so the addition of the freshly ground spice to the finished dish really does make a difference. It also has an important place in confectionery and desserts, pairing especially well with chocolate.

The pungency of pepper's volatile oils generates warmth, first in the mouth and then through the whole body. Its alkaloid piperine also boosts the bioavailability of nutrients. When other spices are combined with black pepper, the piperine helps the body absorb and benefit from their nutrients. Turmeric, for example, is better absorbed when cooked with black pepper and oil.

Black pepper's heat can be harnessed outside the kitchen. Pepper's volatile oils have brought soothing warmth to throat gargles, liniments for the skin, and carminatives to treat gassy digestive systems. Pepper sprays can be used to reduce pests in the garden, and as insecticides against houseflies. These are a cheap, non-toxic and environmentally friendly alternative to expensive heavy-duty chemical sprays which can have unpleasant side effects for all forms of life.

Macadamia (smooth- and rough-shelled)

Botanical names
Macadamia integrifolia
Maiden and Betche
Macadamia tetraphylla
L.A.S.Johnson

Common names
smooth-shelled bush nut,
rough-shelled bush nut,
macadamia nut

Origin and native distribution
Australia (Southern and Southeast
Queensland and Northern
New South Wales)

Parts used
seeds

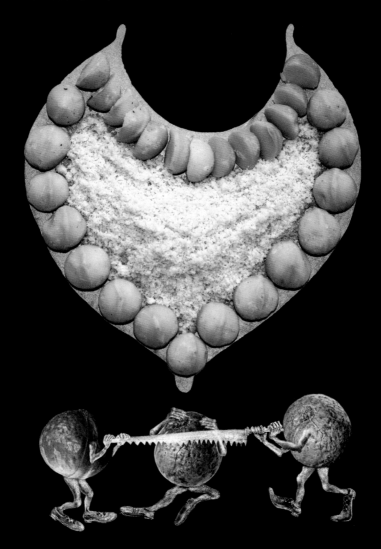

Above: halved and ground macadamias. Below: the two main species
of whole smooth-shelled *Macadamia integrifolia* (left) and rough-shelled *Macadamia
tetraphylla* (right, centre). Both species have shells hard as bone.

Macadamia
- *Macadamia integrifolia* and *Macadamia tetraphylla*

You keep your skeleton inside your skin, it never sees the light.
But nuts wrap ours, called shells, around our flesh so pale and bright.
My creamy sphere is full of fat, a taste that's sweet and mild.
My oil can soften skin and keep it supple as a child's.

My shell is tough to crack, but if your strength can get you through
You'll win the most delicious nut; the most expensive too.
When lands are vast or made of islands dotted through the sea,
It costs a lot to visit, and that's been the case with me.

At first North East Australia was my home; I was unique.
I fed the people of the land; I grew by field and creek.
Then white men came and traded, but took land and freedom too.
For John Macadam I was named, and claimed as something new.

The 1890s took me far; so many centuries
I'd spent at home and now Hawaii held me in its breeze.
My evergreen grew well, content, lapped by the Pacific.
Now both lands feed me to the world. Let's get more specific:

Tetraphylla is rough-shelled, hard to find, it's far more rare.
Integrifolia is smooth, well known, easy to share.
You'll rarely see the thick green peel that splits when I am grown
Unless, led by the Southern Cross, you pick me for your own.

Both *Macadamia integrifolia* and *Macadamia tetraphylla* are evergreen trees which originated in the tropical forests of northeastern Australia. Cream-coloured flower clusters are followed by round fruits with thick green peel which splits open when ripe to reveal the pale brown shell, containing its seed or nut. The smooth shells of *Macadamia integrifolia* and the rough shells of *Macadamia tetraphylla* are hard as bone, so the nuts are shelled before being sold.

Macadamias have the highest fat content of all tree nuts, making them deliciously sweet and buttery with a crisp texture. The nuts of *Macadamia tetraphylla* are higher in sugar and lower in oil content, making them even sweeter. Macadamias are eaten raw, roasted, fried, salted, coated with chocolate, used in confectionery, baking and ice cream, as well as in curries. Macadamia nut oil adds flavour to salads, stir fries and other dishes. The high fat content of macadamias makes their oil valuable as a skin softener or treatment for skin conditions.

Among the indigenous Australians, macadamias provided a symbolic, as well as a nutritional resource. They played a valuable role in the relationships between tribes. At important ceremonial events such as corroborees, when different tribes gathered together, macadamias were traded between tribes and offered as gifts. The oil pressed from the nuts was used to paint clan symbols on the face and body, mixing the oil with clay and natural ochres to create different colours.

The nuts were gathered by women in curved dishes called coolamons, or in dillybags woven from plant fibres which were used to collect and carry food. Once roasted, the nuts would keep well and sustain the tribe on long journeys. The indigenous Australians also valued macadamia as a support to lactating mothers; the newly germinated nuts, still bitter, were eaten to stimulate the production of breast milk.

Once Australia had been colonised by Europeans and its natural resources commercialised, the nuts which had been eaten for thousands of years by the indigenous peoples became the first Australian food plant to enter the international market. In the 1890s, macadamias were introduced to Hawaii, which became an important commercial producer. Today, even with additional growing areas in North and South America and South Africa, macadamias remain a small and therefore expensive crop.

Rosaceae family
Quince

Botanical name
Cydonia oblonga Mill.
Common name
quince
Origin and native distribution
Middle East
Parts used
fruits

Ripe quince fruits still showing patches of downy hair on the skin.
Their flesh will change colour in the cooking pot.

Quince - *Cydonia oblonga*

Quinces are golden pear-shaped fruits
On orchard trees with Persian roots.
Yellow when ripened on the bough,
Pink when jellied, and this is how.

Warm me and I'll flush with pleasure,
Dusky red, a sweetened treasure.
Cooking is a chemical pact:
A magic-science double act.

Heat gives colour where there was none,
Anthocyanin pigments run
Once they've awakened in the dish;
Fire makes yellow blush, as you wish.

In Portuguese we're *marmelo* -
The first true marmalade, you know.
Our pectin helps your jams to set:
Without its strength they'd be too wet.

Our fuzzy skin should not be peeled;
It's where our fragrance is concealed.
Quince paste has names in many lands
Membrillo, cotognata, and...?

Cydonia oblonga is part of the rose family, the third most important *Rosaceae* group after apples and pears; medlars are also part of this family which evolved around 50 million years ago.

When grown in warm sunny regions, quince become soft and sweet enough to be eaten straight from the tree, but in cooler climates the fruits remain hard and astringent. When cooked the heat softens their stony flesh into a more yielding mouthful. Heat also transforms their colourless phenolic compounds into anthocyanin pigments, which give the flesh and cooking liquid a beautiful blushing pink or dusky red tint. This occurs to a lesser degree in pears.

The blushing quince has had romantic associations from ancient times. They are sometimes considered to be the golden apples of the Hesperides in Greek mythology; the fruit given by Gaia to Hera as a wedding gift when she married Zeus. The golden apples were also associated with the goddess of love Aphrodite, or Venus in the Roman pantheon, and have been an official wedding food for over two thousand years. In Jewish and Christian mythology quince is a less celebratory fruit. Along with apples, figs, and others, it has been associated with the Tree of Knowledge which the serpent tempts Eve into eating, after which she and Adam are expelled from Paradise.

The majority of quinces are made into preserves, jellies, conserves and pastes as their high pectin content promotes setting or "jelling". The Persian quince jam is called moraba-ye beh. In Spain and Catalonia a pink sweetmeat made from quince is known as dulce de membrillo and is often served with cheese; similar quince pastes from Italy, Greece and France are known as cotognata, codonyat and cotignac.

In Portugal, quinces are known as marmelo and are preserved by being sweetened and slowly cooked into a thick paste called marmelada. In the 17th century the British borrowed this name and attached it to their breakfast preserve marmalade, which is traditionally made from Seville oranges or other citrus fruits.

Quince was a traditional remedy for constipation, so be careful how many you eat.

Apple

Botanical name
Malus domestica (Suckow) Borkh.

Common name
apple

Origin and native distribution
Middle East

Parts used
ripe fruits

Apples are the world's most widely cultivated fruit trees, and this ripe apple represents just one of thousands of varieties, each with unique flavour characteristics

Apple - *Malus domestica*

Apple of Avalon, apple of Eve,
Apple of Helen, in you I believe.
The sweet growing core of the story is you.
Myths can deceive, but you've always been true.

The crunch and the flavour, the juices that flow
Over skin smooth or mottled, with green or red glow.
A sharp or sweet fragrance in fruit and in flower;
Wassailing we come to anoint you this hour.

And here I await you, celebrants through the years.
You've come to me laughing, you've come flowing tears.
You've come stroking my bark and praying for wealth,
As I've held you in boughs and in blossom; in health.

Four thousand years ago, apple orchards were being cultivated by the Hittites, whose empire spread over modern-day Turkey and Syria. Our eating apples are considered likely to have come from species crossed in the mountains of Kazakhstan, which were carried into Europe by the Romans. The ancient Greeks knew how to graft apples, and developed named cultivars. Over time, several thousand named varieties were established in the temperate regions of the world.

Apples are the most widely cultivated fruit trees, but despite their continued popularity there has recently been a loss of diversity. Many of the smaller, less glossy varieties, whose mottled skin conceals their nutritional and flavourful character, are at risk of being lost. Countries where apples traditionally grow in abundance and variety are importing apples from thousands of miles away, creating a generic and limited (albeit consistent) supermarket menu.

Many apples have a tart freshness thanks to the malic acid that balances out their natural sugars, but apples are being increasingly selected for sweetness. With less malic acid, apples' nutritional content is shifting from fruit to confectionery. Some supermarkets have added the insult of labelling small apples as "fun size", a term only previously used for bars of tooth-decaying chocolate and candy, denying them their varietal name altogether. Seeking out varieties with a tart-sweet flavour is a way to ensure that an apple a day still keeps the doctor and dentist away.

The *Malus* in *Malus domestica* derives from the Latin for *bad*. Was it an apple in the Garden of Eden that caused so much trouble? Other contenders for the fruit of the Tree of Knowledge are apricots, quince, pomegranate and fig. Apples have had a starring role in mythology, folklore and history; from ancient Greece and Rome, to Avalon in the Arthurian legends of Britain, to the story of Isaac Newton being hit on the head by a falling apple, helping him to theorise about gravity.

Apple varieties are broadly classified as suitable for cider, cooking, and eating. Any apples can be used for cider, although more acidic varieties are usually preferred. Bramley apples are a well-known cooking variety. There are many delicious and delightfully-named varieties that don't make it into the supermarkets, but can be found at farmers' markets, in gardens, and in the wild. The wood of the apple tree is the most popular choice for smoking foods, as its flavour is sweet and not harsh. Apple peel tisane is drunk throughout Turkey. As well as being eaten fresh, apples are widely used in cooking, including apple sauce, pies, cakes, and stuffings. Apples are pressed for juice, and fermented to make cider, applejack, and Calvados. The flowers can also be made into fritters, and apple blossom honey is valued for its delicate aroma and flavour.

Almond

Botanical name
Prunus dulcis (Mill.) D.A.Webb

Common name
almond

Origin and native distribution
Central Asia, Middle East

Parts used
seeds

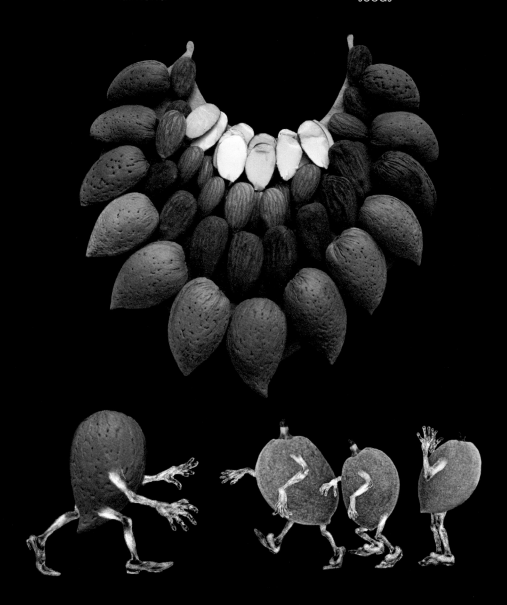

Above: the lower almonds are still in their shells, showing the
variation in shape and surface texture, the inner nuts are un-shelled and
the sectioned nuts show the creamy white flesh.
Below: a hard-shelled mature almond greeting the tender,
edible immature drupes.

Almond - *Prunus dulcis*

To make a medieval dish
Take all the almonds that you wish,
Finely grind them into paste
With sugar, then to lift the taste
Add rosewater; pour drop by drop
Until your nose tells you to stop.
That's *marchpane*, but it's not complete
Until your eyes, too, have a treat.
So press it in a rose-shaped mould
And paint it with bright red and gold.
Then to the banquet you may go
To serve your liege lord, bowing low.

The modern sweetmeat, marzipan,
Is the updated version and
Has been dressed up in chocolate.
But let's explore the real, raw, nut.
Sweet almonds are *Prunus dulcis;*
The most grown of all nuts on trees.
Bitter almonds, *amara*, can
Make cyanide, to kill a man.
They give us almond extract too,
And small amounts are good for you.
But don't munch bitter almonds raw
Or you'll be writhing on the floor.

We're often told that too much sweet
Is not the wisest thing to eat.
But almonds clearly demonstrate
That sweetness should be on your plate.

When is a nut not a nut? Almonds, along with several other tree nuts, are not technically nuts but drupe seeds. Unlike the hard shell of a genuine nut, a drupe has a fleshy outer layer, inside which is a pit containing the seed. With almond's blushing stone fruit relatives such as peaches, cherries and apricots, we eat the fruit around the pit. With almonds and other nut-resembling drupes it's the seed that we eat, discarding the flesh or husk and the pit.

The almond gives two opportunities for eating as it has two ripening periods. The entire drupe can be eaten a few weeks after the blossoms have faded; the fruit is still green and the rind tender. This young almond drupe is a delicacy in the Middle East and some Mediterranean countries. Three months later it comes to maturity when the ripe seed inside has swelled, its covering has become a hard shell, and the outer rind has dried, shrivelled and split. This allows it to fall from the tree; almonds are also harvested by hand or by mechanical shakers.

The almond is native to Central and Western Asia, was domesticated by the Bronze Age and has been cultivated for at least 3,000 years. Today it is the world's largest tree-nut crop despite the challenges in producing a harvest, and California is the biggest producer. The almond is an early bloomer among orchard trees, putting out its blossom in late winter and early spring. This makes it vulnerable to damage by frost; its Hebrew name is *shaqed*, which means *hasty awakening*.

Almonds would have been seasonally important among native peoples for their calorific value due to their high protein levels and calcium content. To protect its seeds from being eaten the ancestral almond produced bitter-tasting chemicals. As humans planted seeds from the mildest trees the flavour became sweeter in character, giving us the sweet almonds we enjoy today. Only now, we are the ones who add the bitter taste of chemical defence to our food.

The almond seed that we eat is enclosed in a pit which ranges from soft-shelled, semi-hard to hard. Almost all of the Californian almonds grown are soft-shelled, making it easier to extract the seeds in preparation for sale. Most European almonds are semi-hard to hard-shelled. The harder the shell, the tastier the seed inside, but these seeds are also smaller. Commercial growing focussed on yield and ease of production has led to the superior hard-shelled almonds becoming less popular. However, harder shells also protect the edible seed from environmental contaminants such as pesticides that are sprayed on the trees. The seeds of soft-shelled almonds will have absorbed a chemical cocktail before they reach our mouths and digestive systems.

Selecting for profitable traits such as large, sweet seeds and uniform size makes almond cultivation easier, but the loss of natural genetic diversity exposes the crops to other problems. When all crops share the same traits, few will escape or prove resilient to an infection, reduced soil quality or other potential harms. Cases of salmonella in Californian almonds in the early 2000s led to the United States Department of Agriculture's controversial decision to ban the sale of raw almonds in the United States. Now all almonds sold, including those labelled "raw", are in fact steam pasteurised or fumigated with propylene oxide (PPO).

Pollination is also managed like a military operation: due to the dramatic loss of bees and other pollinators in the environment, they must be conscripted. Almost a million hives (close to half the beehives in the USA) are transported from other states to California each February to ensure the year's harvest. Due to the worldwide fall in insect numbers, the agricultural industry needs to find pollinator-friendly solutions to ensure the future supply of food crops we have come to rely on.

When buying almonds and almond milk, we can consider the varieties, growing and processing methods that we have to choose from. Organic almonds will be less heavily sprayed while growing; they may still be steam pasteurised but not fumigated after harvest.

Due to the almond's traditional associations with fertility and weddings, sugared almonds, which originated in the Italian town of Sulmona, are a common wedding favour. Marzipan is made by grinding almonds into paste and adding sugar; it is often eaten on its own, formed into shapes and coloured or covered in chocolate. Marzipan is also used in stollen and to form a layer between rich fruit cake and its icing, especially in Christmas and wedding cakes.

Pear

Botanical name	**Origin and native distribution**
Pyrus communis L.	Europe, Western Asia
Common name	**Parts used**
pear	fruits

Left to right: comice and conference, two common varieties
of pears comparing their figures.

Pear - *Pyrus communis*

Apples and pears; we always come second.
Less fêted than apples but sweet, so sweet.
Juicy flesh filled with stone cells, sandy textured,
Will rasp on your tongue like a cat's rough lick.

Pyrus communis, first taken in hand
Four thousand years back. From Asia's broad arms
The swift Romans marched us through Europe's lands,
Planting and scattering cores as they walked,
Fermenting juice into perry for fun,
Later distilled into something more strong;
Brandy to keep our fruits well for winter.

Come, learn my seasons and each season's names:
Bartlett, Bon Chrétien, Williams, Bosc,
Conference, Comice, Winter Nellis, Anjou.
Sweet, but rough-tongued; there's a mystery for you.

Pears originated in Europe and Western Asia. The Romans helped to spread pears throughout Europe, and they are the second largest tree crop in temperate climates after their relative the apple.

Pears have been cultivated in China for 4,000 years, and the Asian pears are known as "sand pears" for their gritty texture. Although they are round and juicy, they are less full-flavoured than the European varieties, which were bred for a smoother texture by French and Belgian growers in the 18th century. All pears have a slight grittiness in their dense flesh thanks to their stone cells, which are hard cells with thick walls.

Like most apples, pears are prone to oxidisation, their pale flesh swiftly turning brown when exposed to the air; a squeeze of lemon juice helps to prevent this. Pears are also badly affected by carbon dioxide, which affects the ripening process, so they should not be stored in plastic bags where the gas can accumulate. As one of the least allergenic foods, pears are often included in food for weaning babies, and are helpful for people on exclusion diets.

Different varieties of pears ripen in different seasons. More than a thousand cultivars exist today, and pear trees can live up to 300 years, a longer life than apple trees. Many of the most common varieties today such as Conference, Doyenne du Comice and Williams are relatively young, introduced less than 300 years ago.

Pears are eaten fresh, served with cheese, pickled, dried, poached in wine, canned, used in baking and desserts, and cooked with meat. Their juice is drunk fresh. Perry pears (comparable to cider apples) tend to be smaller and harder, and have a high tannin content. They were known to the Romans, who fermented them to make perry, a practice which continues today. Perry can then be distilled into brandy or liqueur.

Rubiaceae family
Coffee (arabica and robusta)

Botanical name
Coffea arabica L.
Coffea canephora
Pierre ex A.Froehner

Common names
coffee arabica
and coffee robusta

Origin and native
distribution
Ethiopia, Eastern Africa

Parts used
seeds

Top to bottom: dark roasted, medium roasted and unroasted coffee beans
form a stimulating pattern on a base of ground coffee.

Coffee - *Coffea arabica* and *Coffea canephora*

Between tea and me there has been some rivalry,
But now I'm on the upside of history.
Who'd think my red fruit with two small seeds inside
Could earn billions or be a gourmet source of pride?
Ethiopia and Yemen grew me first of all;
South American beans have today's world in thrall.

Advertisements boast of arabica beans
But they never confess in these marketing schemes
That it's altitude, time in the cool damp thin air,
That develops my flavour beyond all compare.
Coffea canephora gets barely a mention
For beans called robusta, but pay some attention
To decaff and blends as it's there you will see
Robusta's strong bitterness being set free.

When my rich roast aroma curls into your nose
Your brain will do somersaults, fresh as a rose
That has sipped from the sweet morning rain and is waking;
But too much of my caffeine could leave your hands shaking.
So learn moderation; do yourself a favour
And rather than quantity, enjoy the flavour.
Slow right down to sip me and don't rush around
With a takeaway cup; rest your feet on the ground
As you sit yourself down with a book or a friend
To have memories of me at the busy day's end.

A relative of gardenia, the coffee plant originated in the highlands of East Africa. What we call coffee beans are actually seeds. The tree's fragrant white, star-shaped flowers are followed by round drupes or coffee cherries containing two small green seeds. The green cherry changes to red or purple when ripe for picking. The seeds are extracted by machine and dried before being roasted.

Coffee is now cultivated worldwide in the belt between the two tropics. The regions that drink the most coffee; Finland, Scandinavia, Italy, Turkey and North America; do not have suitable climates to grow it. Coffee-drinking nations have developed their own characteristic ways of preparing and serving the drink, and some have special words to describe it. The Swedish tradition of *fika*, a cup of coffee and something sweet to eat, is an important social ritual.

The two most commonly cultivated types of coffee are *Coffea arabica* and *Coffea canephora* which are known commercially as arabica and robusta. *C. arabica* is the oldest known species and is native to the cool highlands of Ethiopia and the Sudan, and is known for its complex and balanced flavour. The closer this species gets to the equator, the higher the altitude needed for optimum growth and quality. Altitude gives a combination of cloud moisture, cold nights that let the trees grow slowly, and volcanic soil rich in minerals that boost flavourful acidity. Arabica beans are mostly larger than those of robusta and have a longer, flatter shape. *C. canephora* species are larger trees that can tolerate higher temperatures than arabica, making them more suitable for growing at lower altitude. They produce the smaller, hump backed robusta beans which have a higher caffeine content than the arabica.

Ripe coffee cherries attract mammals, birds and insects looking for food. To defend itself the plant produces the natural insecticide caffeine. Its bitter taste and powerful effect on the nervous system deters many small predators, but humans have come to crave these sensory spikes. Coffee activates the pleasure centre in the brain in the same way as opium and cocaine.

At first coffee was a solid mouthful rather than a liquid one; the berries and leaves were chewed as a stimulant. In Ethiopia, where cooking with coffee cherry flour was also common, this caffeinated chewing gum is still used today. Coffee as a beverage has its roots in Yemen, where in the 1400s it was drunk in the Sufi monasteries to enhance alertness and spiritual sensitivity during long nights of prayer. The word coffee originates in the Arabic *qahwah*; the Arabs removed the beans from the surrounding cherry and roasted them before adding water.

Thanks to trade and pilgrimage routes coffee became a desirable and expensive commodity once it had gained popularity outside the monasteries. Ethiopia swiftly adopted the new practice of drinking coffee through strong trading links across the Red Sea. The Ethiopians also dried and infused the leaves into a drink still enjoyed today. The Yemeni port of Mocha became an important coffee trading capital and its name is echoed in the Moka coffee pot and the drink combining coffee with hot chocolate. By the early 1500s coffee had travelled across the Arabian Peninsula, into Egypt and the Levant, and up to Istanbul, the Ottoman capital. A hundred years later coffee had spread all the way to Morocco in the west and India in the east.

The first coffee house opened in Istanbul in 1554 and the first in England was "Angel" in Oxford, opened by a Turkish Jew in 1650. Throughout Europe and the Middle East men would meet in coffee houses to drink and discuss current affairs. Women were excluded. It was not uncommon for coffee houses to be closed by anxious Ottoman sultans and European monarchs or infiltrated by their spies, as they were considered hothouses of political and ideological dissent harbouring poets, philosophers and politicians. There was revolutionary potential in these egalitarian tinderboxes where people could conspire over a stimulating but non-alcoholic drink. With coffee, you don't fall over on your way to smash the system.

The rapidly escalating demand for Yemeni coffee and the money to be made by controlling the trade led to political power struggles. First the Ottomans attempted to ban the export of coffee to Europe, then in the 1700s the Dutch, Spanish, British and Portuguese established coffee plantations in their colonies where the use of slave labour ensured a plentiful and affordable supply. These colonial coffees were also exported to Ottoman regions, creating a demand for coffee which was cheaper than the Yemeni original.

Like chocolate, coffee was first drunk black. As new methods of preparing coffee arose over the centuries they did not fully displace the old methods. Coffee may be served hot or cold, black or with milk or cream. Kopi luak is the civet coffee of Asia, especially Vietnam; it is made from beans picked out of a civet cat's faeces and is highly prized. For a less scatological cup, coffee can be flavoured with spices, fruits and florals.

Chilli pepper

Botanical name
Capsicum annuum L.

Origin and native distribution
Central America, South America

Common names
chilli, bird chilli, cayenne pepper

Parts used
fruits

A garland or ristra of fresh red chillies gleaming with mischief.
Ristras are traditionally made with dried chillies and used for decoration.

Chilli pepper - *Capsicum annuum*

I'm *Capsicum*, chilli, the world's favourite spice.
I can play sweet, but even when fiery I'm nice.
In the Americas, Central and South,
I'm known for my oil that sticks to your mouth.
That's why my heat tingles and lingers so long,
Inspiring Rob Johnson to write a new song.

My capsaicin oil sticks to fingertips too,
So get those hands soaped before using the loo.
Yes, *before* not just after, and don't touch your eyes.
You really do not want that kind of surprise.
Maya Indians knew just how fierce I could be,
And sprayed chilli juice straight at their worst enemy.

Some people now think that it's terribly brave
To eat hotter chillies than they actually crave.
My revenge will be sending them home to their Mum
With a burning hot mouth and a scorching red bum.
It's capsaicin oil flowing through the digestion
That makes them regret giving in to suggestion.

It's natural to be curious about my great heat,
And many varieties are purely a treat.
You can crunch up my sweet peppers quite merrily;
Enjoy hot chillies bottled or popped in a curry.
Just explore step by step and don't be a hero;
I promise your street cred will go down to zero
If you start the night stating that you have no fear
And end it in tears putting ice on your rear.

The *Capsicum* species contains thousands of chilli and pepper varieties with a full range of taste experiences. Sweet bell peppers give a juicy crunch to salad, while at the other end of the scale one risks hospitalisation.

Humans have been eating *Capsicum* fruit for at least 10,000 years. It is native to South and Central America, with many varieties known to the Aztecs, and it was used as food, spice and medicine. Columbus brought *Capsicum* seeds to Europe in 1493, and within 50 years *Capsicum annuum* varieties had been planted in the Portuguese colonies in Africa, India and Asia. They were integrated into the regional cuisines and flourished into an important trading commodity. Chilli is now the most beloved spice in the world, accounting for a quarter of the world's spice market.

Chilli is one of the few foods to be weaponised, and the Maya Indians threw a kind of pepper spray at their enemies in battle. Pepper spray is used today as a weapon of submission by the police in some territories. It's the capsaicinoids (mainly capsaicin) that cause this reaction. This chemical compound is found highly concentrated in the white pith and to a lesser extent in the seeds of the pungent chilli varieties. Capsaicin increases an animal's metabolic rate, causing sweating, increased blood flow to the skin and a burning sensation. Capsaicin is the plant's defence system against animals whose chomping teeth would crush the life-storing seeds. Humans, being contrary creatures, have learned to love the pain. Birds swallow the seeds whole, so they travel through their digestive system and emerge intact. In this way they help the plant disperse its seeds, and in return they can eat the fruits without suffering.

While onions release their tear-inducing chemicals into the air when cut, chillies transfer their pungent heat by touch, usually when food enters the mouth. Capsaicin oil clings to skin. It *really* clings. Chilli choppers can wear protective gloves, or use plenty of soapy water to remove this oil from their hands before touching their eyes or other sensitive parts. Chilli's tingling or burning effect makes its journey through the digestive system an adventure from start to finish, as our entry and exit points are richly furnished with nerve endings.

Increasing blood flow to an area can reduce muscular pain, so creams containing capsaicin or pepper extract have been recommended for arthritis, rheumatism and neuralgia. There is also a theory that the brain responds to the burn of the chilli by releasing endorphins, the painkilling chemical compounds that can also give pleasure.

In 1912, a pharmacist named Scoville developed the scale we use today to measure the pungency of chillies, as the ability to tolerate their heat varies from person to person. Scoville Heat Units (SHU) measure by how much a chilli extract has to be diluted in sugar syrup before its heat becomes undetectable to a panel of expert tasters. The sweet bell pepper you'd use in a salad is risk-free at 0 SHU. New Mexico green chillies at 1,500 SHU are mild compared to the chillies at the hottest end of the scale, which exceed 80,000 SHU. However, the Infinity Chilli powers past them all in excess of 1,000,000 SHU. It's the Everest of the *Capsicum* world and can be just as dangerous.

Drying chillies increases the concentration and complexity of their flavour; the chipotle chilli is smoke-dried. The combination of chilli and chocolate goes back to a traditional drink of the Maya. The classic Italian pasta sauce arrabiata blends chilli with its relative the tomato, and with garlic. The Mexican dish chilli con carne is now cooked in many countries around the world. Chilli also works well in contrast, as when cool watermelon is sprinkled with chilli and salt.

The sweet *Capsicum* varieties are rich in vitamins A and C. Both pungent and sweet Capsicums have twice as much vitamin C as citrus. Bell peppers and other large varieties can be filled, raw or cooked, as well as chopped up into salads, sliced as crudités, cooked as vegetables, or used in soups, sauces, and relishes. The smokiness of paprika flavours Hungarian goulash, and paprika itself can be sweet or more spicy.

Capsicum annuum can be easily confused with *Capsicum chinense* (a cultivated species) and *Capsicum frutescens* (which includes the tabasco variety). These three species can look similar and they share a common genetic ancestry, so they are sometimes called the "annuum-chinense-frutescens complex". *Capsicum* continues to evolve as it cross-pollinates easily.

Cape gooseberry and tomatillo

Botanical name
Physalis peruviana L.

Common names
Cape gooseberry, poha,
Inca berry, Peruvian ground cherry

Origin and native distribution
South America (Andes)

Parts used
fruits

Botanical name
Physalis philadelphica Lam.

Common names
tomatillo, Mexican ground cherry,
tomate verde, jam berry

Origin and native distribution
Mexico

Parts used
fruits

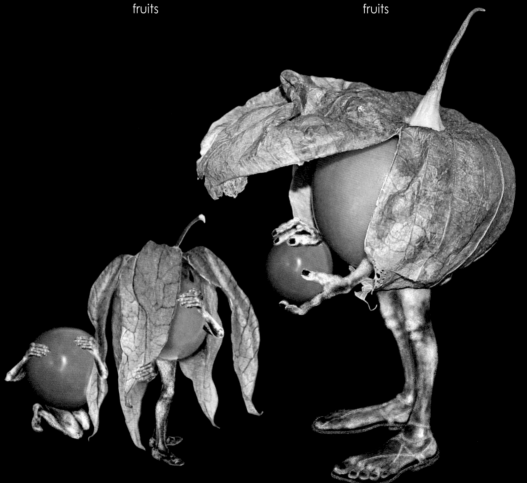

The papery husks shield the small orange globes of Cape gooseberries,
Physalis peruviana, and the larger green tomatillo,
Physalis philadelphica - except when the poor fruit lose their hats.

Cape gooseberry - *Physalis peruviana*

A lantern glimmering in a fairy procession;
A globe glowing orange through a papery husk;
A sweet-tart fragrant surprise with your cheesecake.
Physalis peruviana, whisper it, physalis.

Ground cherry they call me as I fall to the earth,
Gathered in Inca times, and today
For perfumed preserves or chocolate-dipped treasures.
Physalis peruviana, whisper it, physalis.

Tomatillo - *Physalis philadelphica*

Wending their way through the cool hilly highlands
The Aztecs would pluck my green fruit in its husk.
Unripened, my sourness in hot salsa verde
Is mixed with green chilli and brought to the feast.

You'll find me in many a Mexican dish,
Both ripe and unripened according to taste.
Where tomatoes would work you can try me for flavour
Uncooked, or softened a while over the flames.

Cape gooseberry - *Physalis peruviana*

Gleaming through its papery cover like a lantern in a fairy procession, this is a perfumed *Midsummer Night's Dream* of a fruit. The sibilant hiss of *physalis* recalls the whisper of the husk when handled. Outside its native South America, *Physalis peruviana* is more often a garnish than the star of a dish. It adds lustre to a dessert plate with the magical glow of its orange globe, guarded by the delicate Chinese lantern husk. The fruit has a complex sweet-tart flavour combining floral and fruity notes. When the fruit dries naturally on the plant the resulting "raisin" is not high in sugar, but is tasty. The common name of ground cherry comes from the low-lying plants which grow to around one metre in height. The husk dries to a papery texture and provides a handle for dipping the fruit into chocolate, icing and fondant. The fruit can be eaten uncooked, dried and preserved, used in pies, jellies, jams, compotes, sauces, cakes and tarts, and fresh fruit salads.

Although one of its common names is Cape gooseberry, it is no relation to the European gooseberry *Ribes uva-crispa*. The exact origins of that name are debated; the cape could refer to the cape-like husk, or it could allude to the fruit being grown in the Cape of Good Hope in South Africa around the time it was introduced into England. *Physalis peruviana* has high vitamin C and vitamin A content, similar to that of citrus fruits. The fruit is widely used in traditional Andean medicine, and by other cultures worldwide, to treat digestive disorders, cataracts, and a range of diseases and physical conditions. Recent studies into its pharmacological properties show it is an effective antioxidant, strengthening the immune system and acting to remove the free radicals that can cause cancer. Other edible relatives such as *Physalis philadelphica* share these properties, so perhaps it is time to give these underutilised species more space on our plates.

Tomatillo - *Physalis philadelphia*

This green fruit was cultivated earlier than the tomato which it resembles. The Aztecs grew it in the cool highlands of Mexico and Guatemala. It grows inside a paper lantern or husk, an attractive protective feature that distinguishes the *Physalis* species. The sour unripe fruits of tomatillo are used in the traditional meat accompaniment salsa verde, a mildly hot sauce made with green chilli. Salsa verde is often served with tacos, enchiladas, tostadas, chile rellenos and other Mexican dishes such as mole verde. Like the tomato it can be fried, stewed, baked, used in dressings and cooked as a vegetable in curries, soups and stews. The ripe fruit is sweet enough to be eaten out of hand. It is sliced for sandwiches and salads, used in pies and preserves, and occasionally in sweet dishes. Like the chilli pepper the fruit is often hung in garlands or ristras.

Solanaceae family
Tamarillo

Botanical name
Solanum betaceum Cav.

Common names
tree tomato, tamarillo,
tomate de árbol

Origin and native distribution
South America (Andes)

Parts used
fruits

Ripe fruits of the tree tomato or tamarillo showing their
glossy skin and seeded interior.

Tamarillo - *Solanum betaceum*

My name is a bit of a mystery.
Where did it come from? Just listen to me.
In Sixties New Zealand I was named *tamarillo*.
Who decided? I don't know the name of the fellow
Or if it was more a committee affair.
It was done to make me highly prized at the fair.
I mean to help sell me. They gave me this name
To replace *tree tomato*. It's a bit of a shame.
Tree tomato so perfectly says what I am:
A high-growing fruit for both salad and jam.

Just imagine you've travelled across to the Andes;
Argentina, Bolivia; and now that your hand is
Feeling its way up through soft glossy leaves
And finding a warm sunny palmful of me.
Egg-shaped but my colour is orange or red,
Or yellow, or striped, or near-purple instead.
My crops keep on growing the whole year through
So as well as good taste I make good money too
For the people who grow me, but it's such a shame
That they gave me this new, but less sensible, name.

Common names of plants tend to arise from within the culture that uses them. Whether it's a sensory description, a clue to how it is used or was discovered, the names people choose for their everyday eatables express an intimacy with them. In the rare case of tamarillo the name was decided by committee in a marketing push.

Mr W. Thompson of the New Zealand Tree Tomato Promotions Council suggested linking the Maori word for *leadership*, *tama*, with the Spanish word for *yellow, amarillo*, in a name that echoed both the language of the plant's native South America and its new home. The fruit had been promoted during World War II when it was not possible to import fruits such as bananas and oranges, but in the 1960s they were eclipsed by the growing popularity of the kiwifruit. The original yellow, purple and longitudinally striped tamarillo varieties can still be found but New Zealand also developed a new red variety, which is now the most commonly known.

In Ecuador the tamarillo is known as *tomate de árbol*, which translates as *tree tomato*. That makes perfect sense; the fruits grow on an upright shrub of up to five metres in height. It's rich in iron and vitamins A, B6, C and E, and low in calories. Sweeter cultivars of this acidic fruit have been grown to suit the modern palate. Yellow fruits are sweeter while the red is more tart and savoury. Due to this spectrum of flavours, tree tomato can be added to almost anything and cooked in a variety of ways. In Ecuador, their tomate de árbol is made into a hot sauce, aji, with the pungent addition of chilli, and is offered alongside many dishes throughout the Andean region. Throughout South America its juice is used in a refreshing drink, blended with milk, ice and sugar. Ripe fruits are eaten out of hand, used in fruit salads, green salads, sandwiches, soups and stews, and can be made into jellies and jams. Unripe fruits are used in curries and chutneys.

Despite its versatility and nutritional content, having comparable health benefits to tomatoes, this fruit has yet to gain the same international popularity. It's a resilient fruit which can be stored for up to 10 weeks, and each plant can bear 20 kilograms of fruit in a season that can extend all year round, making it a reliable crop for growers in tropical regions and higher elevations of tropical zones.

Solanaceae family
Tomato

Botanical name
Solanum lycopersicum L.
Common name
tomato
Origin and native distribution
South America, Central America
Parts used
fruits

Large beef tomato slipping off its travelling shoes and taking centre stage to tell the story of how humans carried tomatoes to almost every culture in the world.

Tomato - *Solanum lycopersicum*

BOO! Are you scared? Are you sure that you're not?
Well that's good; you seem like a sensible lot.
Europeans got awfully flummoxed and spooked
When they first glimpsed this nightshade - no, not even cooked
Would they try me for almost two hundred whole years!
The Aztecs must have laughed themselves into real tears
To think that these pale-faces searching for gold
Were scared by my fruits - and they thought they were bold!

So give thanks to those first munchers, hungry and brave,
Who sank teeth into me but escaped from the grave.
Solanum lycopersicum, that's how I'm known
Among botanists; call me tomato at home,
An echo from Aztec *tomatl*, you know.
The poetic Italians say *pomi d'oro*
Which means *golden apple*; I have other names too
That a little research will uncover for you.

Now when coming to eat me I have a request.
Keep me out of the fridge to find me at my best.
I don't like being cold, it just makes me uptight
And I'll squeak and go watery and tense with the fright.
So my cherries and buffalos, my plums and my vines,
My sauces and ketchups and garlicky pies
Are all yours for the eating and full of good flavour,
But the fridge doesn't suit me, so do me that favour.

When the tomato arrived from South America in the mid-1500s it was greeted with suspicion by those in Europe with a botanical education. The flower structure was similar to the *Solanaceae* species deadly nightshade and mandrake, whose poisonous nature was well known. The botanists' assumptions robbed Europe of two centuries of rich tomatoey goodness. It was the illiterate peasantry who eventually proved the tomato was worth eating, as well as growing as a decorative climber. The tomato is indeed a nightshade, but a nutritious relative which releases cancer-averting properties when cooked.

Due to their low sugar content most ways of eating tomatoes are savoury, and they generally need a little sugar to even out their acidity. One of the oldest ways of eating tomatoes is in catsup or ketchup, with versions going back to the Aztecs, but modern mass-market recipes would be unrecognisable to the original creators. Some ketchups are not based on fresh tomatoes but on concentrate, and use modified starches to give the appearance of "real" tomato sauce while using up to 25% less real tomato paste.

Real tomatoes reward us with a complex mouthful of vitamins, carotenoids and flavour. There are many tomatoes to try; fruits range from small round cherries to large, weighty beefs, with many round, egg, oval, or plum shapes in between. Some tomatoes are lumpy rather than smooth globes, such as heritage varieties with their longitudinal bulges.

When tomatoes are given time to ripen on the vine, still rooted in the soil and looking at the sun, they become more full of flavour by producing the gaseous plant hormone ethylene, which hastens the ripening process and converts their starch to sugar. Unfortunately, supermarkets often have their tomatoes bred for appearance rather than flavour and picked while green. Cold storage is used to transport unripe green fruits long-distance and extend the shelf life of easily-bruised ripe fruits, but it degrades their flavour. Before they appear in public they are treated with synthetic ethylene gas to make them blush as though they had ripened naturally.

In the commercial practice of prioritising a clone-like regularity of appearance and extended shelf life, offering the consumer just a few well-behaved hybrids, much genetic diversity is lost. We cease to benefit from the plant's innovative ways of getting itself eaten and its seeds dispersed; the eye-catching colours and shapes, and the moreish flavours that heirloom varieties have in abundance.

Tinned tomatoes have their shelf life lengthened with ascorbic acid, or with citric acid (E330). You might assume that this is lemon juice or another plant lending a helping hand, but it is often synthetic additives classed as "processing aids". Currently, these can be legally included in foods without being specifically labelled as an ingredient. They are more strictly regulated for organic tinned foods such as tomatoes.

Manufactured citric acid (MCA, different from natural citric acid) has not been scientifically studied to prove its safety when ingested in quantity. What is proven is that 99% of the world's MCA is produced using the fungus *Aspergillus niger*, which is a known allergen. It's a dance of downward spirals, cutting costs for companies and cutting quality for the consumer. It seems that we have reason to distrust our tomatoes once more; or rather to question the ways they, and therefore we as the eaters, are being manipulated by the invisible and undeclared adulteration of our food.

Aubergine

Botanical name
Solanum melongena L.

Common names
eggplant, aubergine, brinjal

Origin and native distribution
Tropical Asia

Parts used
fruits

Varieties of *Solanum melongena*, including the classic
white oval which inspired the common name of eggplant.
Aubergines vary widely in size, shape and colour.

Aubergine - *Solanum melongena*

Give me fat, give me flavour, I'll soak it all up,
I'm like a big purple-skinned sponge.
My skin can be squeaky, my flesh full of air
But I'll melt in the heat - turn it up!

I've a warm, smoky taste when my outsides are charred
To make a great baba ganoush.
Why eggplant? Well sometimes I'm small, white and oval,
So that explanation's not hard.

In India I'm praised as king of vegetables,
You'll find me all over that land.
Most nightshades hail from the Americas; I'm rare,
Melongena is genuine Old World.

Now whatever you call me, and whether you buy me
In white, purple, or other hues,
Please take my advice and add plenty of spice,
And have that oil hot when you fry me.

The aubergine or eggplant is indigenous to India, where it is known by many names, including brinjal and the "king of vegetables". This makes the aubergine the only major vegetable in the nightshade or *Solanaceae* family to come from the Old World. While nightshades grow on almost every continent (with the unsurprising exception of Antarctica), it is the Americas that have provided the world with the most famous *Solanaceae*: potato, chilli, tomato and tobacco.

Growing year-round and adapted to different climates, aubergine is an important source of income for small farmers in India. From around 500 BCE it was also grown in China, and travelled along trade routes to Arabia and Persia. Arabian traders introduced the aubergine to North Africa and Spain in the Middle Ages, and it gained popularity in Europe.

It's thought that the first aubergines English speakers met with were the small white egg-shaped varieties, inspiring its common name of eggplant. These are mainly grown in Asia today. Aubergine's fruits can be swelling oblong or slim sausage shapes, with glossy hues in purple, white, and green and with some striated cultivars. They are most commonly seen in shades of purple from bright to almost black.

Aubergines are sponges for fat and flavour, soaking up sauces while releasing their own creamy-bitter taste and bolstering a dish with their flesh. They can be cut into chunks in stews, sliced and grilled as steaks, or halved and stuffed. Under the sleek, thin but tough skin of the aubergine lies a pale interior with small bitter seeds, and it is botanically classed as a berry. Its spongy texture arises from air pockets between the cells of the flesh. These collapse when cooking and the flesh melts into yielding silky mouthfuls.

Aubergine is a wonderful vessel for punchy spices like chilli or pungent garlic, as well as for subtle flavours like fragrant cardamom. When flame-grilled or roasted in a hot oven the flesh takes on a rich smokiness. For the Middle Eastern mezze dish baba ganoush this smoky flesh is mixed with garlic, lemon juice, olive oil and tahini (sesame seed paste). Dishes such as ratatouille, melanzane alla parmigiani, caponata and moussaka rely on the aubergine, and it excels as a main course, side dish, dip, sauce and pickle. Slices of aubergine can be used to wrap other foods or rolled into parcels and baked in sauce, and in the Middle East the dried skins are also revived in water and used as vessels for other ingredients.

Solanaceae family
Naranjilla

Botanical name
Solanum quitoense Lam.

Common names
naranjilla, golden fruit of the
Andes, lulo, Quito orange

Origin and native distribution
South America (Andes)

Parts used
fruits

A whole fruit of naranjilla or lulo, whose flavour balances between sweet
and acidic, admiring the golden-green interior of its companion.

Naranjilla - *Solanum quitoense*

Solanum quitoense, naranjilla, that's my name.
I'll tantalise your eyes, your tastebuds and your fingers.
The short brown hairs covering my orange glow
Can be rubbed from my skin when I'm properly ripe.
Hairs are rare among smooth *Solanaceae*.
I'm sometimes called golden fruit of the Andes.
Inside I'm pulpy, juicy and green.
Tomato, pineapple and orange tastes meet in my flesh.
I'm chosen for jams, jellies, sherbets and ice cream.
In Columbia and Ecuador they say I'm like pineapple and strawberry
As they squeeze my juice for their sorbete.
In Panama they prefer me in a lively chicha,
Mixing my liquid with sweet sugar cane.
Have you ever seen me around your place?
In the markets, look out for my bright, bearded face.

This plant with pale lilac flowers bears unusually hairy fruits for a member of the *Solanaceae*. Inside the thick, bright orange skin is the fruit's greenish pulpy flesh. This has a subacid flavour, described as a combination of orange, pineapple and tomato. In Columbia and Ecuador, where naranjilla's freshly squeezed juice is made into green foamy drinks known as sorbete, the flavour is likened to a sweet-sour blend of pineapple and strawberry. In Panama it is combined with sugar cane juice to make unfermented chicha. Naranjilla is also used to flavour ice cream and sherbets, and is made into jam and jelly.

Solanaceae family
Potato

Botanical name
Solanum tuberosum L.
Common names
potato, papa

Origin and native distribution
South America (Andes)
Parts used
tubers

New potatoes making themselves presentable for your plate. Soil
naturally clings to root crops, and not all are thoroughly scrubbed
before being sold. Illustration inspired by Arthur Rackham.

Potato - *Solanum tuberosum*

Don't eat me raw, and don't eat me green,
And don't eat me when I have sprouted.
At all other times I'm a wonderful find
Buried down in the earth: please don't doubt it.
I give most of the nutrients humans desire,
Just a few can't be found inside me.
But adding some dairy redresses this lack
So you have a true food friend in me.

My vitamin C has a habit of fleeing
In air and in pan water too.
So cut me up late, don't make me vegetate
In a pool - put me straight in the stew!
You can bake me and fry me, mash me
And try me in dishes both fancy and plain.
I was carried by ship all the way from Peru;
The Atlantic's too wet for a train.

Solanum tuberosum, what does that mean?
Well, a tuber's a storehouse of starch.
It may take some cooking, but you won't be looking
For snacks while you're out on a march.
A tum full of potatoes will not cost the earth
But will help you to get your work done.
So at your mealtime halt, just sprinkle some salt,
And I'll give energy for your fun.

Potatoes are native to South America and were domesticated in South Peru and Bolivia (near Lake Titicaca) around 8,000 to 10,000 years ago. When the Spanish, Portuguese and English crossed the Atlantic in search of territory, riches and novelties, potatoes came sailing back to a curious Europe, reaching Spain by 1537 and Ireland by 1566.

Potato is an important staple, the world's fourth largest crop after wheat, rice and maize. In the 1500s the peasantry quickly came to rely upon it. Potatoes reduced the chronic malnutrition among the poor of Europe in the 18th century, which contributed to a rapid population expansion. So essential did the potato become in Ireland that when the potato blight fungus struck in 1845 it caused a terrible famine, leading to a huge Irish migration to the USA around 1850. Part of the problem was the lack of genetic diversity in the country's crops, which were "lumper" potatoes and essentially clones of one another. The lack of variety meant there were no islands of resistance that could have saved lives.

In South America, many cultivated varieties are traditionally raised along with wild potatoes. There are around 4,000 varieties of potato, but modern intensive monoculture farming prioritises just a few varieties which give high-yield crops. This leaves the whole system, and all of us who depend on it, vulnerable to catastrophe from drought, pesticide resistance or new diseases. Farmers, whether small or large scale, need long memories: it is diversity that will keep people fed.

The potato provides almost all the nutrients needed by humans (with the exception of vitamins A and D). It is a storehouse of energy because it is, literally, a storehouse; the tuber is stocked with vitamin C, vitamin B1 (Thiamin), potassium, fibre, protein and carbohydrate. Eating a variety of plants, including different kinds of potatoes, helps humans to stave off illnesses thanks to the complex combinations of chemicals that strengthen our immune systems.

White, red, yellow and purple potatoes offer a range of flavours to be discovered. They can also be eaten throughout the year; new (immature) crops in spring and summer and mature in autumn, and they store well in the cool dark for the lean months of winter. Potatoes can also liven up dark times through their role as a fermenting agent for chicha and beer, or by being distilled into vodka or the Scandinavian drink aquavit, which is flavoured with fragrant spices including cardamom, caraway, and orange or lemon peel.

Potatoes are part of the nightshade family, relatives of the tomato, sweet bell pepper, chilli and aubergine, which reads like a meal in itself. Also in this family is tobacco, which can also be chewed, but ideally not in the same mouthful as its relatives.

Along with their nightshade siblings within the genus *Solanum* the potato plant contains significant levels of glycoalkaloids like solanine and chaconine. These protect the plant from diseases, insects and animals. In the edible tubers, they are increased by exposure to light and insufficiently cool storage. Potatoes that have sprouted, turned green, or taste bitter after cooking should not be eaten, as this indicates a high and potentially toxic level of these natural defences. In most cases it can be enough to remove the skin and cut out the sprouted parts, but if in doubt it's best to discard a potato if it has sprouted tentacles.

You can get along very well knowing only the two main textures of potato: floury or waxy. Knowing what kind of potato you have in your hand can decide for you the question of what to do with it; generally a choice of cooking in water, in dry heat, or in hot oil. Floury potatoes contain more dry starch, and the cells swell and separate when cooking, making them go fluffy. They are best dressed with fat and milk or cream, so are ideal for mashing, frying, roasting and baking. Waxy potatoes can be cut into pieces without collapsing during cooking, so they are perfect for gratins, potato cakes and salads where a potato can provide substance. All potatoes are suited to salt.

Tea

Botanical name
Camellia sinensis (L.) Kuntze

Origin and native distribution
Subtropical Asia

Common names
tea, chai

Parts used
leaves

Top to bottom: Different stages of tea. The same plant
is processed differently to produce white, green, jasmine pearls,
tag teas, oolong and black tea.

Tea - *Camellia sinensis*

Discover the perfect pot of tea,
A fragrant, pure, clear-eyed cup.
Or tannin-deep darkness as rich as a stew,
Leaving brown rings when you're washing-up.
Perhaps you are craving the chlorophyll punch
Of green matcha, ceremoniously whisked.
Or is it yak butter, a pinch of bright salt
That will perk up your kidneys a bit?
Kombucha's fermented; its tight streams of bubbles
Shoot straight to the surface, all blinking.
A samovar saves boiling time and those troubles;
It holds a whole day's worth of drinking.
As for sugar, that sweet delight has tea to thank
For its rapid ascension and status.
Tea loaves, lumps and crystals have all had their hour
As the sweetener of tea's bitterness.

You could float a lemon slice, vivid and sour,
Or drown in the comfort of milk.
You might infuse the brew with the scent of a flower,
Or essential oils pure as raw silk.
A cup and a saucer, a mug or a glass,
A thermos or hand-painted chalice?
A sip or a stomach full, what's in your hands
In the woods, at your desk, in your palace?
I'm not really asking, I don't want debate
Or to challenge your taste or tradition.
If my perfect cup brings you out in a frown
It's a preference; it's hardly sedition.

Theaceae family

From China to India's green terraced hills;
That's where *Camellia sinensis* began.
With opium, silver, and old-fashioned greed
Tangled up in competitive plans.
Green, black or oolong; leaves always desired
First for health then for wealth and for power.
Meditating on emptiness, Japanese monks
Taught the world not to rush the tea hour.
Revolution stirred up in America showed
One should not underestimate tea.
When you sit calmly sipping so gently, in peace,
Float your mind through its wild history.

Now, today, pop the tea caddy lid to reveal
Scented separate leaves, flaking soft.
Or pick up a tea brick so dense that a hammer
Heaves down to smash smithereens off.
That tea bag protecting your eyes from the truth -
Are there leaves held inside, or just dust?
And if there is plastic and bleach in the cloth
Could that mean you have misplaced your trust?
There's plenty of power in water when boiling
To draw out the goodness - just so
It will also disperse in your favourite drink
Little bits of - you'd rather not know.

After water, tea is the most commonly consumed liquid on the planet. Humans have been drinking tea since around 3000 BCE, and may have chewed the leaves before recorded history. All the different teas - black, green, oolong, white, yellow and Pu'er tea - are from the same plant, *Camellia sinensis*. Their different characteristics and flavours are a result of different processing methods and which parts are picked.

In the wild, tea plants can grow up to ten metres high, but in plantations they are kept trimmed to below one and a half metres for ease of harvesting. Only the terminal bud and two or three young leaves below it are used, but there can be four flushes a year.

The young tea leaves contain more psychoactive material, and the growing altitude is important. On higher hills the bushes grow more slowly and experience a greater difference in temperature between day and night, and they release stronger yet less bitter flavour compounds in response. The bitterness of polyphenolic compounds and alkaloids such as caffeine are the plant's natural defence against insects, and the proportion of pests decreases as the altitude and cold increase. By growing tea at insect-resistant altitudes the need for artificial pesticides is reduced, and the result is a healthy leaf which gives complex flavours without excessive astringency.

Tea was first prepared as a medicine; it has antibacterial and antioxidant properties and a high vitamin C content, as well as naturally occurring fluoride for healthy teeth and gums. Tea contains 2% to 4% of the psychoactive alkaloid caffeine which, along with its astringent taste, can refresh the mind; too much can be over-stimulating and prevent sleep.

By 708 CE tea had become a staple in China; in addition to its health benefits, drinking boiled water was safer as it reduced the chance of intestinal problems if the water was contaminated. In 805 CE tea was introduced to Japan as a medicine. In the 12th century, Japanese Buddhist monks developed tea drinking into a formal ceremony, considering the beverage not only an aid to study but deserving of contemplation in its own right.

Tea reached Europe in the 16th century, brought back from China by travellers. Britain developed a costly demand for the drink which it funded by growing opium in its colonies and selling it to Chinese merchants. When the Chinese government objected to the societal damage caused by the opium trade the British declared war on China and soon afterwards established tea plantations in its colonies in India, where the native teas of Assam were also domesticated.

It was the late 17th century before tea reached America via Europe. The British government's tea tax of 1767 increasing the burden of previously imposed taxes gave impetus to the American Revolution, which resulted in the Declaration of Independence in 1776.

The year 1904 brought two major American innovations in tea drinking; iced tea was offered at the 1904 World's Fair in St. Louis, and tea bags were invented. Thomas Sullivan, a New York tea and coffee shop merchant, used small muslin bags to send samples of his tea blends to customers. Discovering that they could pour boiling water directly over the bag without extracting the messy leaves, Sullivan's customers ordered so many tea bags that a special machine was developed to pack them.

Until the late 19th century all the world's tea was China tea. Two principal tea varieties are used today. The small-leaved Chinese variety plant (*Camellia sinensis* var. *sinensis*) is hardier, growing in the cool elevations of southern China, Darjeeling, and the Himalayan foothills. The large-leaved Assamese plant (*Camellia sinensis* var. *assamica*), used mainly for black tea, is more suited to the warm climates of Sri Lanka and Assam where the British established their rival plantations during their conflict with China.

Garden nasturtium and mashua

Botanical (and common) names
Tropaeolum majus L.
(garden nasturtium, Indian cress)
Tropaeolum tuberosum Ruiz and Pav.
(mashua, tuber nasturtium, anu)

Origin and native distribution
South America (Andes), Peru

Parts used
(garden nasturtium) flowers,
leaves, seeds (mashua) tubers

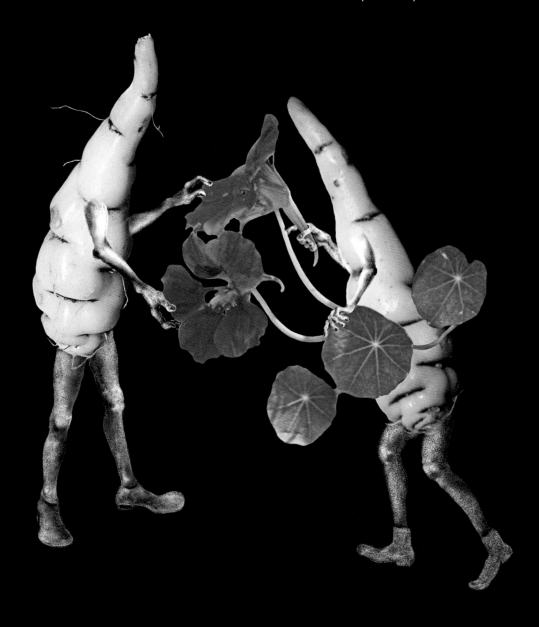

Two species of nasturtium: the conical tubers of *Tropaeolum tuberosum*
admiring the peppery leaves and bright flowers of *Tropaeolum majus*.

Garden nasturtium - *Tropaeolum majus*

My open-mouthed flowers are bold and bright,
My leaves and seeds fill salads with delight.
With peppery fire to give you a thrill
From Peru, to your greenhouse or windowsill.

Mashua - *Tropaeolum tuberosum*

Before pesticide sprays were invented
The farmers would use other plants,
Interspersing the crops and creating
A healthy bug-resistant dance.
Some food plants produce their own chemicals
That insects can't stand to be near,
So crops hand in hand with bug-scaring friends
Give better yields, year after year.
At home in the Andes, mashua's my name;
My tubers are dried, boiled and munched.
My leaves and my flowers are edible, but
Not everyone wants me for lunch.
Since Incan times soldiers have used my flesh
To focus their minds on the fight,
Forgetting temptations of love at home;
Tubers cool passion and calm fright.
But modern men who feel invincible,
Yet don't want to risk finding out
If a meal could muddle their potency,
Hide from me in the safety of doubt.

Garden nasturtium - *Tropaeolum majus*

This plant was brought to Europe from Peru in the late 17th century and proved popular thanks to its bright yellow, red, and deep orange blooms. These edible flowers make inviting additions to salads, and the flower buds, leaves and seeds are also eaten. The leaves have a hot peppery taste similar to watercress, and can be used to wrap food parcels as well as added to salads and vegetable dishes.

The common names for garden nasturtium and tuber nasturtium come from their shared flavour profile with watercress (*Nasturtium officinale*), which is a member of the mustard and cabbage family. The mature seeds of garden nasturtium are eaten raw or roasted, and can be ground like pepper. The flower buds are used like capers when pickled. The plant is high in vitamin C.

Mashua - *Tropaeolum tuberosum*

Across the Andean regions of Peru and Bolivia, at altitudes too high for potatoes to grow, *Tropaeolum tuberosum* or mashua is a valuable resource. This plant is also an example of how different species can protect one another through companion planting. *Tropaeolum tuberosum* contains high levels of glucosinolates which function as an insecticide, preventing crops from being ravaged by the tiny creatures and diseases that can cause enormous damage. When interspersed with other plants they act as protection for the entire crop. They are also easy and quick to grow even in poor soils, and they give a generous yield of tubers so they are a profitable and secure choice for farmers.

For humans, the glucosinolates in mashua have medicinal benefits. In traditional medicine it is used to treat kidney conditions and as a diuretic. It has shown effectiveness in preventing some cancers. It was historically used by the Incas as an anaphrodisiac during military campaigns, ensuring the soldiers kept their attention on their duties rather than being distracted by desire.

Mashua is a nutritious tuber high in vitamin C, with a peppery taste and vanilla aroma. The tubers are conical and can be red, purple, yellow or white. They can be partially air-dried, boiled, or boiled and then frozen. They are used in stews and as a vegetable, and the leaves and flowers are also edible.

Zingiberaceae family
Turmeric

Botanical name
Curcuma longa L.

Common names
turmeric, Indian saffron

Origin and native distribution
South India, Southeast Asia

Parts used
dried rhizomes

The smooth-skinned, lemon yellow Madras, and the rough-skinned,
dark red-orange Alleppey varieties of turmeric rhizomes reaching up to
the bright glow of the slices and the powdered spice.

Turmeric - *Curcuma longa*

Curcuma longa cannot be dimmed,
A radiant sun, yellow kisses.
One touch and my brightness remains on your skin,
Whether or not you might wish it.

My kisses are healing, soothing hot
Inflammation, blisters or tattoos.
Try India or Polynesia for pots
Of fresh paste made for ritual use.

Dye for wool carpets, silk saris too,
Rice and bold mustard; it's my rhizome
That makes curry powder and dal call to you,
Glowing gold with a warm welcome home.

Turmeric glows with a rich golden-orange colour which stains skin, food and fabric. Its name derives from the Sanskrit word *kuṅkuma*, meaning *yellow*. The ancient ancestor of the cultivated variety has not yet been found in the wild, but it is believed to have been domesticated in India in prehistoric times and India is still the most important producer.

Turmeric is most commonly known as a powdered spice, but can also be used fresh. To make the spice, the underground stems or rhizomes of the plant are boiled or steamed and then sun-dried before being ground. The most prominent commercial varieties of turmeric are the dark red-orange Alleppey, whose root has a rough outer skin, and paler lemon yellow Madras, which has a smoother textured root.

Turmeric's flavour and aroma can be described as musky, woody, dry, earthy, and peppery. It has a delicate bitterness and pungency, sharing some chemical notes with its warmer relative ginger. Turmeric is an essential component of most prepared curry powders, contributing at least 25% of the mix. In addition to curries it is used in prepared mustards, in cheeses, butter, sauces, pickles, and in rice, egg, and fish dishes.

Turmeric is traditionally cooked with black pepper and oil or fat, which improves its bioavailability and enhances its benefits. The colour pigment compound curcumin is a powerful antioxidant and anti-inflammatory, inhibiting the development of some cancers and arthritis. In some parts of Asia, turmeric water is used to promote a glowing complexion. Turmeric has many well documented therapeutic effects and is extensively used in traditional Indian household remedies, as well as to colour the skin, clothes and ritual foods for ceremonies surrounding marriage and death. As turmeric is not very light-fast, you can get rid of accidental stains by exposing the fabric to sunlight.

Turmeric is one of the plant pigments for face and body paint in Theyyam, the traditional tribal ritualist dance of the Dravidians performed in the Kāvû or sacred groves in the north Malabar region of Kerala. In Hindu and Buddhist culture, turmeric's deep yellow is associated with the sun and the abundance it brings. It represents a spiritual connection with the earth in which the rhizomes grow. Turmeric also symbolises fertility, prosperity, and purity.

Turmeric was introduced to Polynesia before Europeans arrived there, and it thrives in tropical regions. It has continued to play an important role in ceremonies and medicine on Rotuma in Fiji, while in Samoa it is used medicinally in coconut oil to treat skin complaints such as blisters, and to soothe pain after traditional tattooing.

Zingiberaceae family

Cardamom and black cardamom

Botanical name
Elettaria cardamomum (L.) Maton

Common names
cardamom, small cardamom

Origin and native distribution
Southern India

Parts used
dried fruits (capsules), seeds

Botanical name
Amomum subulatum Roxb.

Common names
black cardamom, Nepal cardamom

Origin and native distribution
Eastern Himalayas

Parts used
dried fruits (capsules)

Whole cardamoms surrounding their decorticated seeds. The off-white, rounded pods are the aromatic Malabar variety and the green, longer pods are the harsher Mysore variety. Below them is the black or Nepal cardamom, a larger relative with a harsh, smoky flavour profile.

Zingiberaceae family

(Loosely based on the poem 'A Subaltern's Love-song' by John Betjeman)

Cardamom and black cardamom
- Elettaria cardamomum and *Amomum subulatum*

Cardamom bun, cardamom bun,
Is anything tastier under the sun?
Doughy and fragrant, I fill up your mouth
With sweet aromatics from India's south.

Cardamom curry, cardamom curry,
I liquify stressful days, soften all worry.
A comforting flavour whose warmth, never burning,
Relaxes the body and stops the mind churning.

Cardamom coffee, cardamom coffee,
Arabia's prized combination that pours me,
Ceremoniously served in a small painted cup,
Delighting the senses and waking you up.

From the west coast of India I've travelled far;
German immigrants sailed me to Guatemala.
Scandinavians love me for sweetness in baking;
I'm still queen of spices, whatever you're making.

Nepal cardamom is the false to my true,
Large, strong, and much cheaper, it's smoke-dried for you.
Seek delicate Malabar, green woody Mysore;
Pods named for the lands where my heart lies for sure.

Cardamom - *Elettaria cardamomum*

Known as the "queen of spices", cardamom or true cardamom is the third most expensive spice after saffron and vanilla. While cardamom's relatives ginger and turmeric are cultivated for their rhizomes, this plant is grown for its clusters of fibrous three-angled pods or capsules containing many aromatic dark brown seeds. The capsules grow in clusters on thin, branching stems called panicles. As these trail along the ground they must be picked by hand, and this intensive labour makes cardamom expensive to harvest.

Cardamom is native to the evergreen monsoon forests of Southern India, where cultivation is restricted to the Western Ghats. This long chain of hills provides the essential conditions for the plant's growth: an altitude of between 700 and 1300 metres, plentiful annual rains, rich slightly acidic soil, an average temperature between 15 °C to 35 °C, and humidity of 75% to 90%.

German immigrants took cardamom plants to the hills of Guatemala, which is now the largest producer. It is also cultivated in the hilly regions of Sri Lanka, Papua New Guinea and Tanzania.

Cardamom has been traded since at least the 3rd century BCE, joining dried ginger and black pepper as a coveted spice. It was known to Arabic traders, whose voices are echoed today in cardamom's name, which comes from an Arabic word meaning *to warm*. The spice is valued for its subtle, aromatic warmth and sweetness. Beyond this shared characteristic, there are considerable differences in flavour and aroma among different cultivars.

There are three main cultivated types: Malabar, Mysore, and their natural hybrid Vazhukka. Cardamoms from the Malabar group are relatively superior, and are valued for their delicate floral notes. They can be recognised by their small round capsules. The flavour is at its best when the green capsules are turning off-white, and it is usually sun-dried or chemically bleached to ensure the pods are all cosmetically ready for sale. Mysore have more robust eucalyptus and woody notes, and produce elongated capsules. These are generally given a colour-fixing heat treatment before being dried to keep their green vibrant. Vazhukka, though robust, blends the characteristics of Malabar and Mysore.

India and South Asian countries consume a lot of cardamom. Today, the international trade is dominated by the Arab countries, who import around 80% of the world's cardamom to use in their gahwa, coffee made with cardamom. The Nordic countries import another 10%; it is widely used in pastries and baked goods, and in mulled wine.

Cardamom can be used as whole capsules, whole seeds, or ground. It is best to buy the capsules and grind them as needed as the ground spice swiftly loses its aroma; keeping the seeds in their husk preserves their potency and flavour. Whole capsules are used in gahwa, curries and rice dishes. Ground cardamom is found in many curry powders. The spice's versatile aromatics are used to flavour savoury and sweet dishes, sausages, pickles, cakes and gingerbread, and drinks. It pairs well with the earthy sweetness of carrots, sweet potato and squash, as well as with banana, pistachio and cashew. It is popular in traditional Indian milky desserts and sweetmeats.

Black, Nepal or false cardamom - *Amomum subulatum*

Black, Nepal or false cardamom, is used as a cardamom substitute. It is cheaper and shares the eucalyptus notes of the true spice, but also has notes of camphor. This dried fruit is four to six times the size of cardamom, about the size of a nutmeg. When harvested its capsules are red, but after being traditionally smoke-dried they turn dark brown. This process adds a smoky flavour which also distinguishes it from the more delicate aromatics of true cardamom. It is an important ingredient in the Afghan spice mix char masala, and the Indian blend pan masala. It is used in rice and meat dishes, pickles, drinks and sweets, and is produced mostly in West Bengal, the eastern Himalayas of North India, Nepal and Bhutan. India is a major producer and exporter.

Ginger

Botanical name
Zingiber officinale Roscoe

Origin and native distribution
India, Southeast Asia

Common names
ginger

Parts used
rhizomes (young or mature)

These deceptively pale, earthy fragments are forming a circle of fire:
part of a whole rhizome joins sliced and powdered ginger. All carry
significant heat with the power to both stimulate and soothe.

Ginger - *Zingiber officinale*

This is a gingery journey - hold tight!
Beneath my warm fug is fire; don't get a fright,
Just be cautious when using my spice, fresh or dried.
My pungent rhizomes restore health deep inside.

When stomachs are heaving like waves on the sea,
To feel grounded and settled just reach out to me.
Fresh root brewed as tisane will help settle digestion,
And travel sickness? Ginger answers that question.

When colds and sore throats cause trouble and pain,
Get hold of some fresh ginger root once again.
Mix with turmeric, hot water, lemon and honey;
This golden elixir won't cost you much money.

Bite into a gingerbread slice and you'll travel
And taste medieval Europe; time unravels
When we keep historic foods alive and breathing,
So find an old recipe book and get reading.

I'm warm, tasty medicine for everyday.
In stir-fries and curries and drinks you can play
With my flavours that brighten sweet cakes and desserts.
Zingiber officinale for joys and hurts.

For at least 3,000 years, ginger has been cultivated throughout tropical Asia. It was domesticated in prehistoric times and has not yet been found in the wild. Today, India and China are the biggest producers although plantations also thrive in Jamaica, Hawaii and other Pacific islands, Mauritius, and African countries including Uganda, Nigeria and Sierra Leone. Ginger from different regions varies in its flavour characteristics.

As well as being a major world spice, ginger is prized as a shamanic drug believed to have magical properties. It is revered and used in rituals by the Native American Indian peoples, and by shamans on the island of Siberut in Indonesia.

Ginger travelled along the trade routes from India to the Mediterranean in the time of the ancient Greeks. Its name comes from the Greek *zingiberis*, derived from the Sanskrit *singabera*, meaning *horns* or *antlers*, which ginger's branching rhizomes resemble. By the Middle Ages, ginger had become one of the most important spices in Europe, and the first gingerbread dates from this time. In the 19th century the powdered spice was sprinkled over drinks, which led to the invention of ginger ale and beer.

Ginger has a biting warmth and a sweet, fragrant pungency that shines in both savoury and sweet dishes. The rhizomes are used raw, dried, powdered, made into crystallised ginger or preserved in syrup. To make the spice the rhizome is peeled and dried in the sun or by machine. Fresh ginger is sliced or chopped for use in curries, stir-fries, marinades, soups and sauces; it is an important base ingredient throughout Asia. Fresh and dried ground ginger are used in chutneys and pickles as well as in sweet baked goods, confectionery and drinks. In Yemen, ground or grated ginger is added to coffee and makes up to 15% of the total weight.

Ginger is famed for its medicinal benefits as well as its culinary uses. It stimulates the circulation and has a warming effect, explaining its traditional use as an aphrodisiac. It calms nausea and digestive upsets, and is used to treat travel sickness, morning sickness, flatulence and colic. Its warming effect on the lungs makes it a good remedy for chesty cold symptoms.

Index by common names

Achaya, K. T. (1994) *Indian Food: A Historical Companion*. Delhi: Oxford University Press.

Balfour, E. B. (1943) *The Living Soil: evidence of the importance to human health of soil vitality, with special reference to post-war planning*. London: Faber and Faber.

Barber, D. (2016) *The Third Plate: Field Notes on the Future of Food*. London: Abacus.

Berry, W. (2021) *What I Stand for Is What I Stand On*. Penguin Books Ltd.

Betjeman, J. (1973) 'A Subaltern's Love-song', in *John Betjeman's Collected Poems*. London: John Murray.

Blythman, J. (2015) *Swallow This: Serving Up the Food Industry's Darkest Secrets*. London: HarperCollins Publishers.

Bowker, G.C. & Star, S. L. (1999) *Sorting Things Out: Classification and Its Consequences. Parts II and III*. Cambridge, MA.: MIT Press.

Brady, R. (2002) *Perception: Connections Between Art and Science*. Available at: https://www.natureinstitute.org/ronald-h-brady/perception-connections-between-art-and-science (Accessed: 24 April 2021).

Bruneton, J. (1999) *Pharmacognosy, Phytochemistry, Medicinal Plants*. 2nd ed. Andover: Intercept.

Campbell, T.C. & Campbell, T. M. (2006) *The China Study: The Most Comprehensive Study of Nutrition Ever Conducted and the Startling Implications for Diet, Weight Loss, and Long-Term Health*. Dallas, TX: BenBella Books, Inc.

Carson, R. (1962) *Silent Spring*. New York: Fawcett Crest.

Chevalier, A., Marinova, E. & Peña-Chocarro, L. (ed.) (2014) *Plants and People: Choices and Diversity through Time*. Oxford; Philadelphia: Oxbow Books.

Chivian, E. & Bernstein, A. (2008) *Sustaining Life: How Human Health Depends on Biodiversity*. Oxford: Oxford University Press.

Collen, A. (2015) *10% Human: How Your Body's Microbes Hold the Key to Health and Happiness*. New York: Harper.

Crosby, A. W. (2003) *The Columbian Exchange: Biological and Cultural Consequences of 1492*. 30th anniversary ed. Westport, Conn.: Praeger.

Cumo, C. (2015) *Plants and People: Origin and Development of Human-Plant Science Relationships*. Boca Raton, Florida: CRC Press.

Dalby, A. (2000) *Dangerous Tastes: The Story of Spices*. Berkeley: University of California Press.

Davidson, A. (1999) *The Oxford Companion to Food - illustrations by Soun Vannithone*. Oxford: Oxford University Press.

de Guzman, C. C. & Siemonsma, J. S. (eds). (1999) *Plant Resources of South-East Asia. No. 13, Spices*. Leiden: Backhuys Publishers.

Douglas, J. S. (1978) *Alternative Foods: A World Guide to Lesser-Known Edible Plants*. London: Pelham.

Duke, J. A. (2001) *Handbook of Nuts*. Boca Raton, Florida: CRC Press.

Duke, J. A. et al. (2003) CRC *Handbook of Medicinal Spices*. Boca Raton, Florida: CRC Press.

Facciola, S. (1998) *Cornucopia II: A Source Book of Edible Plants*. Vista, California: Kampong Publications.

Goodall, J. & Hudson, G. (2014) *Seeds of Hope: Wisdom and Wonder from the World of Plants*. New York: Grand Central Publishing.

Selected sources

Grieve, M. (1931) *A Modern Herbal: The Medicinal, Culinary, Cosmetic and Economic Properties, Cultivation and Folk-Lore of Herbs, Grasses, Fungi, Shrubs, & Trees with Their Modern Scientific Uses*. 1st ed. Jonathan Cape, London.

Grigson, J. (1998) *Jane Grigson's Vegetable Book, illustrated by Yvonne Skargon*. London: Penguin.

Hamilton, J. (1990) *Arthur Rackham: A Life with Illustration*. London: Pavilion.

Hanson, T. (2015) *The Triumph of Seeds: How Grains, Nuts, Kernels, Pulses, & Pips Conquered the Plant Kingdom and Shaped Human History*. New York: Basic Books.

Heinrich, M., Müller, W. E. & Galli, C. (2006) *Local Mediterranean Food Plants and Nutraceuticals*. Basel; London: Karger.

Holdrege, Craig (2013) *Thinking Like a Plant: A Living Science for Life*. Great Barrington, MA: Lindisfarne Books.

Howard, A. (1972) *The Soil and Health: A Study of Organic Agriculture*. Lexington: University Press of Kentucky.

Janick, J. & Paull, R. E. (eds) (2008) *The Encyclopedia of Fruit & Nuts*. Wallingford, UK; Cambridge, MA: CABI North American Office.

Jeffrey, C. (1973) *Biological Nomenclature, Special Topics in Biology*. London: Edward Arnold.

Laws, B. (2010) *Fifty Plants That Changed the Course of History*. Newton Abbot, Devon: David & Charles.

Lehner, E. & Lehner, J. (1973) *Folklore and Odysseys of Food and Medicinal Plants*. London: Harrap.

Lewington, A. (2003) *Plants for People*. London: Eden project Books.

Lewis, G. et al. (2005) *Legumes of the World*. Surrey: Royal Botanic Gardens, Kew.

Livingston, A. D. & Livingston, H. (1996) *The Wordsworth Guide to Edible Plants and Animals*. Hertfordshire: Wordsworth Editions Ltd.

Mabberley, D. J. (2017) *Mabberley's Plant-Book: A portable dictionary of plants, their classification and uses*. 4th ed. Cambridge, UK: Cambridge University Press.

Maesen, L. J. G. van der. & Somaatmadja, S. (eds) (1989) *Plant Resources of South-East Asia. No. 1, Pulses*. Wageningen: Pudoc Scientific Publishers.

Mancuso, S. (2021) *The Nation of Plants: A radical manifesto for humans*. London: Profile Books.

Margulis, L. (1992) *Diversity of Life: The Five Kingdoms*. Hillside, NJ.: Enslow.

Margulis, L. (1998) *The Symbiotic Planet: A New Look at Evolution*. London: Weidenfeld & Nicolson.

Massal, E., Barrau, J. (1956) *Food Plants of the South Sea Islands*. Noumea, New Caledonia: South Pacific Commission.

McGee, H. (2004) *McGee on Food & Cooking: An Encyclopedia of Kitchen Science, History and Culture*. 2nd ed. London: Hodder & Stoughton.

Moerman, D. E. (2010) *Native American Food Plants: An Ethnobotanical Dictionary*. Portland, Or.: Timber Press.

Parasecoli, F. (2019) *Food*. Cambridge, MA.: The MIT Press.

Pollan, M. (2011) *The Omnivore's Dilemma: The search for a perfect meal in a fast-food world*. London: Bloomsbury Publishing PLC.

Pollock, N. J. (1992) *These Roots Remain: Food Habits in Islands of the Central and Eastern Pacific since Western Contact*. Laie, Hawaii: Institute for Polynesian Studies.

Prance, G. T. & Nesbitt, M. (2005) *The Cultural History of Plants*. Abingdon, Oxfordshire: Routledge.

Prance, G. T. (2022) *Flowers, Fruits and Fables of Amazonia*. Poole: Redfern Natural History Productions.

Ragone, D. (2023) *Breadfruit, National Tropical Botanical Garden*. Available at: https://ntbg.org/breadfruit/ (Accessed: 23 Oct 2023).

Rätsch, C. (2005) *The Encyclopedia of Psychoactive Plants: Ethnopharmacology and Its Applications*. 1st U.S. ed. Rochester, Vt: Park Street Press.

Sams, C. (2003) *The Little Food Book: An explosive account of the food we eat today*. Alastair Sawday Publishing.

Shakespeare, W. (1994) *Hamlet 3.1.65 in the Complete Works of William Shakespeare*. Glasgow: HarperCollins Publishers.

Shiva, V. (1993) *Monocultures of the Mind: Perspectives on Biodiversity and Biotechnology*. London: Zed Books.

Siemonsma, J. S. & Piluek, K. (eds.) (1993) *Plant Resources of South-East Asia. No. 8, Vegetables*. Wageningen: The Pudoc Scientific Publishers.

Simpson, B. & Conner-Ogorzaly, M. (2000) *Economic Botany: Plants in our world*. 3rd ed. Dubuque, Iowa: McGraw-Hill.

Skinner, C. M. (1925) *Myths and Legends of Flowers, Trees, Fruits, and Plants, In All Ages and In All Climes*. Philadelphia; London: J. B. Lippincott company.

Smith, C. H. & Beccaloni, G. (eds.). (2008) *Natural Selection and Beyond: The Intellectual Legacy of Alfred Russel Wallace*. Oxford: Oxford University Press.

Spooner, B. M. & Roberts, P. (2005) *Fungi*. London: Harper Collins Publishers.

Stocks, C. (2008) *Forgotten Fruits: A guide to Britain's traditional fruit and vegetables*. London: Random House Books.

Thomas, D. (1967) 'In the beginning', in *Collected Poems 1934-1952*. London: J. M. Dent & Sons Ltd.

Tripathi, A.D., Darani, K.K. & Srivastava. S.K. (eds.) (2022) *Novel Food Grade Enzymes: Applications in Food Processing and Preservation Industries*. Gateway East: Springer.

Van Wyk, Ben-Erik. (2005) *Food Plants of the World: An Illustrated Guide*. 1st ed. Portland, Or.: Timber Press.

Vaughan, J.G. & Geissler, C. A. (2009) *The New Oxford Book of Food Plants*. Oxford: Oxford University Press.

Wallace, A. R. (1876) *The Geographical Distribution of Animals: With a Study of the Relations of Living and Extinct Faunas as Elucidating the Past Changes of the Earth's Surface*. New York: Harper and Brothers.

WFO (2024) *World Flora Online*. Available at: http://www.worldfloraonline.org/ (Accessed: Jan 2023 - Dec 2023).

Whistler, W. A. (2000) *Plants in Samoan Culture*: The Ethnobotany of Samoa. Isle Botanica.

Wickens, G E. (1995) *Edible nuts*. Rome: Food and Agriculture Organization of the United Nations.

Wilson, E. O. (2001) *The Diversity of Life*. New ed. London: Penguin.

Acknowledgements

The preparation of this book has involved many sources and help from numerous individuals around the world. Valuable contributions have come from food plant enthusiasts and experts ranging from home growers, farmers, and market stall holders to the researchers at The Natural History Museum, London and The Royal Botanic Gardens, Kew, and their libraries.

Thanks to Chris Kendall for feeding us both for many years.

Thanks to all whose professional expertise helped us publish this book.

Vilma Bharatan
Thanks to Monique Le Luhandre and the late Carlos Ohms for their endless support, and for sharing their professional expertise in nurturing and refining my photographic skills. Thanks to Brian Spooner for his patience and generosity in devoting large chunks of his time to proofreading and editorial contributions.

Liz Kendall
Thanks to my friends for their encouragement, and to Candlestick Press and The Hedgehog Poetry Press for being the first to publish my work. Thank you to the inspiring and supportive community at my local poetry open mics. I'm grateful to the late George Timcke for setting a fine example of dedication, generosity, and getting books finished.

To the reader
Thank you for exploring the world of food plants with us. We have a free newsletter community where we share our research, recipes, and more that we could not include in this book. We hope you will join us by signing up at meetusandeatus.co.uk. For more information about us and our work you can visit vilmabharatan.com and theedgeofthewoods.uk.

If you enjoyed *Meet Us and Eat Us: Food plants from around the world* we would appreciate your review. This helps us find new readers, develop our newsletter, and respond to your interests. You can leave a review on our distributor's website, or wherever you buy and review books online. You can also email a review for us to share to hello@meetusandeatus.co.uk.

More copies of *Meet Us and Eat Us* can be purchased direct from our distributor at yorkbookshop.com. You can also order our book from your local bookshop, or online from bookshop.org. If you ask your local library they might also add it to their collection.

Geographical regions for the origin and native distribution of food plants

Origin and native distribution of food plants are not defined by political boundaries. Most plant species can have huge natural ranges. Native distribution describes the indigenous geographical range where the species originated and lived. The exceptions are those cultivated varieties and hybrids which humans have developed. **Middle East** is a term that replaced Near East in the early 20th century. These countries are located primarily in Western Asia, Egypt in Northern Africa, and a part of Turkey in Southeast Europe. **Mediterranean region** refers to the areas surrounding the Mediterranean Sea, including the coastal regions of Western Asia, Northern Africa, Europe and parts of Turkey. **Northeast Europe** includes the European part of Russia, while the rest lies in Northern Asia.

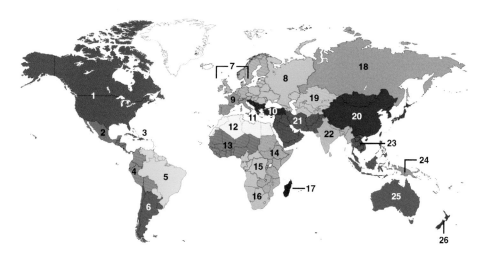

1. North America
2. Central America & Mexico
3. Caribbean
4. Tropical Andes
5. Tropical South America
6. Temperate South America

7. Northwest Europe
8. Northeast Europe
9. Southwest Europe
10. Southeast Europe
11. Mediterranean basin

12. Northern Africa
13. Western Africa

14. Eastern Africa
15. Central Africa
16. Southern Africa
17. Madagascar

18. Northern Asia
19. Central Asia
20. East Asia
21. Western Asia
22. South Asia
23. Southeast Asia

24. Pacific region
25. Australia
26. New Zealand

**We are grateful to our generous Kickstarter patrons who helped us
make this book. Our thanks go to:**

Robin Alabaster
Senthil Ananthan
Patti Baker
Paul Baker
Tessa Barrett
Sue Biggs
Cecile Brich
Liesel Corp
Lisa Coultrup
Juan Carlos Cure
Mark Davidson
Guy Graham
Sharron Green
C J Grübel
Jacqueline Hall
Clive Holmes
Jill Howley
Sean Howley
Anamarta Jade Circle®
Chris Jones
Chris Kendall
Rabeah Kiani
Bernadette T King
Arnie Lord
Kevin Miles
Gretchen Hagen Petrakis
Elaine Phillips
Sarah Slade
Brian Spooner
Mavis A. Stone
Andrew Thorne
David Christopher Ward
Tom Wolseley